LEADING PLCs AT WORK®
Districtwide

From Boardroom to Classroom

**ROBERT EAKER JANEL KEATING
MIKE HAGADONE MEAGAN RHOADES**

Solution Tree | Press

a division of

Solution Tree

555 North Morton Street
Bloomington, IN 47404

800.733.6786 (toll free) / 812.336.7700
FAX: 812.336.7790

email: info@SolutionTree.com
SolutionTree.com

Visit **go.SolutionTree.com/PLCbooks** to download the free reproducibles in this book.

Printed in the United States of America

Library of Congress Cataloging-in-Publication Data
Names: Eaker, Robert E., author. | Hagadone, Mike, author. | Keating,
    Janel, author. | Rhoades, Meagan, author.
Title: Leading PLCs at Work® districtwide : from boardroom to classroom /
    Robert Eaker, Mike Hagadone, Janel Keating, Meagan Rhoades.
Description: Bloomington, IN : Solution Tree Press, [2020] | Includes
    bibliographical references and index.
Identifiers: LCCN 2020028206 (print) | LCCN 2020028207 (ebook) | ISBN
    9781949539714 (paperback) | ISBN 9781949539721 (ebook)
Subjects: LCSH: Professional learning communities. | Team learning approach
    in education. | School improvement programs. | School districts. |
    School management and organization.
Classification: LCC LB1731 .E1285 2020 (print) | LCC LB1731 (ebook) | DDC
    371.2/07--dc23
LC record available at https://lccn.loc.gov/2020028206
LC ebook record available at https://lccn.loc.gov/2020028207

Solution Tree
Jeffrey C. Jones, CEO
Edmund M. Ackerman, President

Solution Tree Press
President and Publisher: Douglas M. Rife
Associate Publisher: Sarah Payne-Mills
Art Director: Rian Anderson
Managing Production Editor: Kendra Slayton
Senior Production Editor: Suzanne Kraszewski
Content Development Specialist: Amy Rubenstein
Copy Editor: Miranda Addonizio
Proofreader: Mark Hain
Text and Cover Designer: Rian Anderson
Editorial Assistants: Sarah Ludwig and Elijah Oates

For Janel

Many years, my trusted friend and colleague

—Bob Eaker

For Jay Hambly

Your standard of care and leadership lessons have left a significant imprint on my life. You have helped me work daily to develop people and make the world a better place.

—Janel Keating

To my wife Sandra and my children Nick, Dan, Courtney, and Cody for their ongoing love and support. My hope is that our grandchildren will be the beneficiaries of the systems and processes that are discussed in these pages. I would also like to share my appreciation for the wonderful mentorship of Bob Eaker and Janel Keating. I wouldn't be here without them leading the way. Finally, I am indebted to the principals and staff of the White River School District. Your tireless work has made a significant difference in the lives of the children we serve.

—Mike Hagadone

For my mother, Aggie Coates, who taught me that everyone has something to teach us if we are just willing to listen, and my father, Ross Coates, who taught me to pay attention to what people do, not what they say.

—Meagan Rhoades

Acknowledgments

We are grateful to the White River School District Board of Education for their leadership and support in the implementation of Professional Learning Community at Work® (PLC at Work) practices within the district. The board gifted us with a weekly one-hour late start for team collaboration and provided resources for ongoing professional development while teams worked to implement PLC concepts and practices. The board's work in establishing focus-area goals connected to student learning data and the four critical questions of learning in a PLC has kept us centered for fourteen years. The work we have accomplished would be nearly impossible without a strong relationship with our labor associations. Their leadership has kept a focus on what's best for students as well as what's best for their membership, and that has made all the difference. We also want to express our appreciation and admiration for the administrators and the staff of the White River School District for their passion, hard work, dedication, and professionalism. Daily, they live the meaning of what it means to be an educator.

It's impossible to overstate the debt we owe to Robert Eaker. He has been a consistent friend to the White River School District, always willing to contribute his years of wisdom to support our journey, a truly priceless gift.

We would also like to recognize the contributions and support of our Solution Tree family. Special thanks to Jeff Jones and Douglas Rife, without whom this book—and much more—would not be possible. From the Professional Learning Communities at Work Institutes to a wide range of top-flight resources to constant encouragement and support, Solution Tree has been a partner on our journey. A special thank you to Kim Bailey, Rich Smith, Doug Reeves, Tim Kanold, Mike Mattos, Luis Cruz, Anthony Muhammad, Ken Williams, Sarah Schuhl, Bill Barnes, and Maria Nielsen—all Solution Tree Associates who have visited the district in an effort to help deepen our professional practice. Simply put, the resources and support from Solution Tree have been a huge factor in our districtwide reculturing efforts. Finally, special thanks to our editor, Suzanne Kraszewski. Her enthusiasm, attention to detail, and probing questions undeniably improved the quality of our book.

Solution Tree Press would like to thank the following reviewers:

Dave Barker
Superintendent
Fremont County School District 1
Lander, Wyoming

Lucas Francois
Superintendent
Waterford Union High School
Waterford, Wisconsin

Lazunia Frierson
Executive Director of Teaching and
Learning
Houston County School District
Perry, Georgia

Felice Hybert
Assistant Superintendent of Curriculum
Kankakee School District 111
Kankakee, Illinois

Margo Kibbler
Board of Education Vice President
Windsor Central School District
Windsor, New York

Jesse Morrill
Principal
Kinard Core Knowledge Middle School
Fort Collins, Colorado

Cecilia Wilken
Director of Teaching and Learning
Ralston Public Schools
Omaha, Nebraska

Visit **go.SolutionTree.com/plcbooks**
to download the free reproducibles in this book.

Table of Contents

About the Authors xi

Introduction 1

    Basic Assumptions About Aligning the Work of Teams Districtwide 1

        Assumption One: Superintendent Leadership Matters—a Lot! 2

        Assumption Two: Leaders Must Connect to the Why. 4

        Assumption Three: Clarity Precedes Competence. 5

        Assumption Four: Team Work Is Aligned Within a Simultaneous Loose and
            Tight Culture 5

        Assumption Five: Leaders Support Teams Through Reciprocal Accountability . 6

        Assumption Six: Leaders Monitor and Celebrate the Work of Teams 6

    The Right Work, the Right Way, for the Right Reasons. 7

    A Cyclical Process 8

        The School Board and Superintendent Team 8

        The District Leadership Team. 8

        The Building Leadership Team 9

        Teacher Collaborative Teams 9

        Data Flow 9

    About This Book 9

    White River School District. 11

    Conclusion. 12

CHAPTER 1

Starting at the Top: The School Board and Superintendent Team 13

    Focus on the Why: Building Shared Knowledge 14

    Engage in Collaborative Teaming: The Engine That Drives White River 16

    Emphasize Expectations and Requirements. 17

        Direction and Clarity From the Top—Goals 18

        Loose-Tight Leadership 19

Process for Establishing SMART Goals...............................20

Expectations for Team Meetings 21

The TACA Process...............................22

Develop a Written Plan..............................29

From *Hoping* to *Planning*..............................29

The Districtwide Planning Process..............................30

The District Calendar 31

The District Planner 32

Scale the Work..............................42

Conclusion...............................46

CHAPTER 2

Setting the Stage: District Leadership Team 49

Principals Must Be District Leaders...............................51

Principals Must Communicate an Accurate and Compelling Why and How......52

The Why...............................52

The How...............................54

Connecting the Why and How 55

Principals Must Know the Work Deeply...............................56

Principals Must Plan, Monitor, and Support Professional Development........60

Include Teacher Leaders: The Building Learning Coordinator 62

Drill Deeper With Focused Teamwork 65

Focus on Principal Leadership 67

Celebrate Successes Along the Journey...............................69

Conclusion...............................71

CHAPTER 3

Leading the Work at the School Level: The Building Leadership Team 73

Create Layers of Leadership 74

Participate in Team Leader Training 77

Lead the Learning...............................82

Establish Clarity About the Work 83

Monitor Team Progress Toward Goals...............................84

Build a Healthy Culture 86

Engage in Cycles of Collective Inquiry and Action Research.................88

Unwrapping Standards...............................88

Setting SMART Goals...............................89

Conclusion...............................90

CHAPTER 4

Improving the Learning: Teacher Collaborative Teams 91

Focus on Controllable Variables 93

Create a Caring and Encouraging Classroom Environment 94

Build a Guaranteed and Viable Curriculum 94

Determine SMART Goals 95

Use Effective, Research-Based, and Affirmed Instructional Strategies 96

Frequently Monitor and Analyze Evidence of Student Learning 97

Monitor and Give Feedback on Products and Artifacts 100

Provide Additional Time, Support, and Extension for Learning 101

Frequently Recognize and Celebrate Accomplishments 104

How Collaborative Teams Function 106

The Role of the Team Leader 106

The Collaborative Team Meeting Process 107

The Unit Plan Skeleton 108

Tools for Team Planning 118

A Platform for Transparent Collaboration 118

Monthly Planning Tool 122

District-Developed Resources for Unit Planning 123

Singletons and Collaborative Work 126

Conclusion 134

CHAPTER 5

Envisioning an Aligned District 137

References and Resources 141

Index 145

About the Authors

Robert Eaker, EdD, is professor emeritus at Middle Tennessee State University, where he also served as dean of the College of Education and later as interim executive vice president and provost. Dr. Eaker is a former fellow with the National Center for Effective Schools Research and Development.

Dr. Eaker has written widely on the issues of effective teaching, effective schools, helping teachers use research findings, and high expectations for student achievement, and has coauthored (with Richard DuFour and Rebecca DuFour) numerous books and other resources on the topic of reculturing schools and school districts into professional learning communities (PLCs).

In 1998, Dr. Eaker was recognized by the governor of Tennessee as a recipient of Tennessee's Outstanding Achievement Award. Also in 1998, the Tennessee House of Representatives passed a proclamation recognizing him for his dedication and commitment to the field of education. In 2003, Dr. Eaker was selected by the Middle Tennessee State University Student Government Association to receive the Womack Distinguished Faculty Award.

For over four decades, Dr. Eaker has served as a consultant to school districts throughout North America and has been a frequent speaker at state, regional, and national meetings.

To learn more about Dr. Eaker, visit AllThingsPLC (www.allthingsplc.info).

Mike Hagadone, MEd, served as the assistant superintendent of White River School District in Washington State until his retirement in 2020. With forty years of experience, he is a former teacher, assistant principal, principal, and director of secondary education.

During his tenure as principal at White River High School in Buckley, Washington, the school was recognized as a Washington Achievement Award winner (2011) and a School of Distinction (2012). White River High School was designated as a Model PLC by Solution Tree in 2015.

Mike was selected as the Washington High School Principal of the Year in 2011 and has served as the president of the Washington Association of Secondary School Principals.

He earned a master's degree in educational administration from the University of Idaho and a bachelor's degree in social studies and secondary education from the University of Idaho.

Janel Keating, MEd, is the superintendent of the White River School District in Buckley, Washington. An accomplished educator with more than thirty years of experience, Janel has served as an elementary and middle school teacher, elementary principal, director of student learning, and deputy superintendent. For eight years, Janel had the privilege of being the principal of Mountain Meadow Elementary School in Buckley, Washington. During her time there, Mountain Meadow was recognized as one of the highest academically performing elementary schools in the state (2004 and 2006). Mountain Meadow is currently the highest performing of nearly 180 elementary schools in Pierce County and a 2020 DuFour Award finalist. Janel has been named Principal of the Year in Pierce County, Washington. In 2019, Janel was the recipient of the Robert Handy Award for the most effective administrator in Washington State. She presents at state and national events, is a coauthor with Richard DuFour, Rebecca DuFour, and Robert Eaker of *The Journey to Becoming a Professional Learning Community*, and coauthored with Robert Eaker the books *Every School, Every Team, Every Classroom* and *Kid by Kid, Skill by Skill: Teaching in a Professional Learning Community*. She has written numerous articles on leadership and school improvement. She coauthored with Eaker the lead chapter in the 2012 Yearbook of the National Council of Teachers of Mathematics. Janel was presented with the 2013 Carroll College Alumni Academic Achievement Award, which is given to alumni who have distinguished themselves academically.

Janel consults monthly with school districts throughout the United States. Since 2005, Janel has shared her thinking to improve school systems, schools, teams, and classrooms with nearly four hundred schools and school districts. She is past president of the Washington State Association for Supervision and Curriculum Development.

Janel earned a master's degree in educational leadership from the University of Idaho and a bachelor's degree in elementary education from Carroll College in Helena, Montana. She received a superintendent's certificate from Seattle Pacific University.

Meagan Rhoades is the district assessment coordinator in White River School District in Buckley, Washington. She has worked in this district for more than twenty years. Meagan came to this position in an unusual way, starting in the district as a substitute paraeducator, then working as a building secretary, and then moving to the district office and working in the technology department. When Janel Keating moved to the district office, Meagan stepped in as her assistant, and from there moved into the assessment coordinator position.

Meagan has presented and copresented at numerous conferences; a personal highlight for her was copresenting with her mother at the National Association for the Education of Young Children conference in 1992. She worked with Robert Eaker to guide the PLC work in his hometown for the Murfreesboro (Tennessee) City Schools. She has also served as a consultant for several school districts and has been a cowriter for Solution Tree blogs and the website AllThingsPLC (www.allthingsplc.info).

To book Robert Eaker, Mike Hagadone, Janel Keating, or Meagan Rhoades for professional development, contact pd@SolutionTree.com.

Introduction

There is ample evidence to support the fact that the Professional Learning Community (PLC) at Work process is not only effective in improving one school in a district but is also a powerful tool for districtwide school improvement. Increasingly, researchers, writers, and practitioners have focused on the role district leadership plays in school improvement efforts. Research by Robert J. Marzano and Timothy Waters (2009) highlights this important role. Education writer and researcher Karin Chenoweth (2015) observes, "District leadership shapes the conditions in which schools operate and as such can support or undermine school success and thus student success" (p. 14). Although the focus of early effective schools research was on the *individual* school, Lawrence W. Lezotte (2011) recognizes the critical role the district office plays in supporting school improvement efforts: "If creating and maintaining schools as effective isn't a district-wide priority, the school will likely not be able to maintain its effectiveness status" (p. 15).

While these and a significant number of other researchers and writers highlight the fact that district leadership and support are critical to school success, there is less information available regarding how PLC concepts and practices must be aligned districtwide to realize the full potential of the PLC process. If educators are serious about improving learning for *all* students within a school district, we must look beyond improving schools one at a time and focus on improved learning from a districtwide perspective. This book is our call to action: it is time to align the work of the district office and the work within and across the entire school district.

Aligning the work of teams, districtwide, to ensure high levels of learning for all students is a complex and difficult undertaking. The challenge is taking what seems like common sense and making it common practice—in every school, at every level, and task by task.

Basic Assumptions About Aligning the Work of Teams Districtwide

A districtwide PLC is more than the sum of its parts. A high-performing district that functions as a PLC reflects a thoughtful alignment of the right work—starting at the top with the school board, then at the district office, next in individual schools, and ultimately in collaborative teacher teams. At each level, support staff take part in collaborative teams and their work is part of this critical alignment. Importantly, the alignment of the work at each level of teaming is based on six critically important assumptions.

1. Superintendent leadership matters—a lot!

2. Leaders must connect to the why.

3. Clarity precedes competence.

4. Teamwork is aligned within a simultaneous loose and tight culture.

5. Leaders support teams through reciprocal accountability.

6. Leaders monitor and celebrate the work of teams.

Assumption One: Superintendent Leadership Matters—a Lot!

In *Raising the Bar and Closing the Gap*, Richard DuFour, Rebecca DuFour, Robert Eaker, and Gayle Karhanek (2010) highlight several powerful actions that effective district leaders take. In their review of districts that had effectively implemented PLC practices and concepts, they found remarkable similarities within these districts. In each of these districts, the superintendent took ultimate responsibility for reculturing the entire district. Sometimes, superintendents had other staff assist, such as an assistant superintendent or director of student learning, but ultimately, without leadership from the superintendent, things simply did not get done. The leadership behavior of the superintendent was key.

Even if the superintendent wasn't immersed in the details surrounding the actual day-to-day work, he or she was encouraging and supportive. And, importantly, he or she insisted that the district collaboratively develop a plan to accomplish data-based improvement goals across the district. Each superintendent took the responsibility for improving the learning of all students—and adults—within the district very seriously. Each superintendent the authors studied realized the need to align all the policies, practices, and procedures with this mission of learning for all. Each superintendent set the expectation that this is the work everyone would engage in doing.

Let's be crystal clear: without the superintendent putting this work of improving learning on the top of the pile—making the alignment of the work a district priority—it won't be possible to effectively implement and sustain the concepts and practices of a PLC district-wide. What the superintendent does daily, and what he or she pays attention to, must send the message that no initiative or task in the district is more important than the learning of both students and adults.

The superintendents DuFour and colleagues (2010) studied utilized the power of building a guiding coalition. The guiding coalition often included a member of the school board, representation from the district office, and building principals. Key teacher leaders and support staff were also an important part of this team. The superintendents spent time ensuring the education and training of the team, which, in each case, ultimately became one of the most influential teams in the district. The *guiding coalition* is responsible for learning about successful PLC practices and concepts, and importantly, making an emotional commitment to join with the superintendent and school board on the journey to becoming a high-performing PLC. The superintendents that DuFour and colleagues (2010) studied gradually built a knowledge and commitment base throughout the entire district. In short, the superintendents featured in *Raising the Bar and Closing the Gap* led the districtwide improvement process, but they did so through shared leadership.

Each superintendent focused on enhancing the leadership capacity and effectiveness of each principal within the district. Most districts chose to improve their schools by focusing on the teaching staff: observing and evaluating teachers, giving them a new instructional framework, and sending them to workshops on effective teaching. What the successful superintendents realized was the school was as good as the principal leading it. The principal needed to be at least as well off—as well-informed and committed—as the teacher teams he or she was expected to lead. Each of the superintendents DuFour and colleagues (2010) studied focused on improving schools by improving principal behavior.

To be blunt: if a principal doesn't understand the PLC concepts, he or she will botch leading the PLC, making it difficult for teacher teams to do this important work, and the work will never be deeply and effectively embedded schoolwide. These superintendents ensured that their principals avoided that by organizing them into a team or teams, depending on the size of the district. The principal teams engaged in deep learning about PLC processes and practices, becoming students of the PLC concept. The goal of the superintendents was to create a cadre of PLC experts at the principal level.

Importantly, principals were required to organize their schools into *collaborative teams*— teams of teachers who teach the same or similar content. They were also expected to direct the work of each team. The superintendents didn't leave what teams did to chance. Teams learned to focus on their planning and work around critical PLC practices.

Teams planned together; they collaborated; they collaboratively addressed issues and questions that were likely to arise; they were transparent about their work, making the products of their work available to everyone else; and most important, they learned together. In short, they functioned as a *high-performing team*, rather than simply a collegial group engaged in random tasks.

Superintendents (and the school board) clearly communicated that they expected principals would enhance the performance of each team within their schools. This expectation formed the foundation of a culture of continuous improvement. Principals needed to do much more than simply communicate expectations from the district office. They had to become deeply involved in the work of each team. Principals accomplished this engagement with the work primarily through establishing a leadership team that consisted of team leaders who met with the principal weekly. This leadership team guided and shared the work that each teacher team was addressing. The expectation that principals were responsible for the ultimate effectiveness of each team not only increased both student and adult learning in the district but also created positive peer pressure.

In each of the schools that DuFour and colleagues (2010) studied, the superintendent had directed each principal to collaboratively develop and share with others in the district a plan to provide additional time, support, and extension of learning. The plans needed to meet a few basic criteria: time, support, and extension of learning must occur within the school day, and be available for all students—regardless of the teacher to whom students were assigned. The plan must be timely, providing time, support, and extension of learning no later than two weeks into the school year. Students must not miss core instruction in order to have access to additional time, support, and extension of their learning except in the most extreme circumstances. And finally, the plans had to be directional rather than invitational—that is, they directed students to receive additional time, support, or extension of their learning rather than simply inviting or encouraging them to do so.

In each of these districts, the superintendent also expected principal teams to do the same work that they expected of others. This had a dramatic effect on how principals conducted meetings. Principal teams anticipated issues and problems, practiced and rehearsed the work that they would expect of teacher teams, and shared learning data. In other words, the district office principal team was engaged in the same work the team expected of its individual schools' collaborative teacher teams. *They were learning by doing.*

In addition to focusing on the principals, the superintendents monitored and celebrated the work at every level in a frequent and timely manner. They didn't assume that just because people *did* the work that they were doing the right, high-quality work. They monitored the work as if it mattered. And, they didn't just monitor yearly—an annual "Did you reach your goals?" approach. They monitored the work as it was being done, unit by unit, and importantly, they celebrated improvement of both individuals and groups, both students and adults, along the way.

Finally, these superintendents made a commitment to limit new initiatives. PLC was not one of many approaches to school improvement; rather, it was *the* approach to continuously improving learning within the district. Superintendents viewed the PLC process as an overarching process under which educators would use best practices to improve student learning, based on the collaborative analysis of data, collaborative goal setting, and collective inquiry into what those best practices should be. In this sense, the PLC process was an ongoing, cyclical process that drove continuous improvement—year in and year out. And, simply put, schools cannot effectively establish or maintain such actions absent effective leadership from the superintendent and the district office staff.

Assumption Two: Leaders Must Connect to the Why

Aligning the work of teams within a PLC requires much more than restructuring the work that teachers and administrators do within the district; aligning the work requires that everyone understand *why* they are being asked to engage in various tasks and activities. People are willing to work hard if they feel the work is worthwhile. Successfully aligning the work requires motivation, inspiration, energy, enthusiasm, and the articulation of a clear and compelling purpose. As Simon Sinek (2009b) reminds us, great leaders inspire everyone to take action by starting with, and frequently referring to and answering, the question of "Why?"

What is the why in a PLC? Why should leaders work so hard to align the work of every team, every day? The answer is clear: to ensure high levels of learning for all students—grade by grade, course by course, subject by subject, unit by unit, lesson by lesson, skill by skill, and name by name.

Leaders of PLCs inspire others by frequently reminding everyone of the district's mission of improving the learning of every student. The why is the cornerstone of aligning the work in a PLC; every major step on the school improvement journey requires reminders of the why. Why are educators being asked to do what they are doing, and why is doing it so critically important? What educators do every day makes a difference and can change lives, and they need leaders to help them remember that.

Assumption Three: Clarity Precedes Competence

Even if district leaders expect alignment of the work from the district office to the classroom, success will depend on common understanding—clarity—among everyone involved. Mike Schmoker (2004) reminds us that "clarity precedes competence" (p. 85). Aligning the work, team by team, task by task, involves a deliberate effort to ensure a common understanding, and a common vocabulary, that forms a common foundation for the work ahead.

Leaders must not assume that everyone has the same understanding of terms such as *common formative assessment, summative assessment*, and *collaborative teaming*, or even what it means to be a PLC. Equally important, leaders must realize that one workshop, one book study, or one handout will not suffice. Clearly articulating concepts and terms must be a thoughtful, deliberate, and ongoing process. Being informed is not the same as having a deep, rich understanding of concepts and terms. As Michael Fullan (2005) puts it, "Terms travel easily . . . but the meaning of the underlying concepts does not" (p. 67).

Clarity also involves being clear and concise regarding expectations. Educators can feel inspired by the why, but they might still be confused about the what. Principals and teacher teams need a clear understanding of exactly what it is they are being asked to do. Ambiguity leads to frustration, and frustration has a negative impact on quality. Principals and teacher teams need to know the time frame for when to do the work. They need high-quality examples of the work that leaders expect of them. Also, teams benefit from clear, collaboratively developed standards of quality. That is, leaders should determine beforehand what the completed task or product should look like if completed at a high level of quality.

Assumption Four: Team Work Is Aligned Within a Simultaneous Loose and Tight Culture

Thomas J. Peters and Robert H. Waterman (1982) in their classic work *In Search of Excellence: Lessons From America's Best-Run Companies* advocate an approach that is both loose (encouraging experimentation, autonomy, empowerment, and creativity) and tight (having non-negotiables in areas such as organizational mission, vision, core values, and commitments).

When Peters and Waterman (1982) studied some of America's best-run companies in order to determine what leadership practices they had in common, they found that each of the companies reflected a culture that was both loose and tight. Marzano and Waters (2009) refer to this approach as *defined autonomy*. Regardless of the term, the power of experimentation, creativity, and empowerment within tight boundaries cannot be denied (Eaker & Sells, 2016).

The simultaneous loose-tight leadership approach leads to the questions, How loose and how tight? The fundamental challenge of district leadership is the too-loose, too-tight dilemma (DuFour & Fullan, 2013). They point out that successful district leadership does not require less leadership at the top, but rather more—*more of a different kind*.

Effective superintendents create a culture that gives focus and direction for the tasks at hand, while at the same time encouraging empowerment, autonomy, and creativity. Simultaneous loose-tight leadership is an essential tool for creating such a culture.

Assumption Five: Leaders Support Teams Through Reciprocal Accountability

Teams need resources and support to effectively implement PLC concepts and practices, what Richard F. Elmore (2004) refers to as *reciprocal accountability*. At its most basic level this means that as leaders expect certain tasks and products of others, they have an equal responsibility to provide the capacity to meet those expectations. Teams need resources such as training, materials, suggestions, and most important, high-quality examples. And each team must have feedback, encouragement, and support. Just like students, adults—and groups of adults—learn at different rates and in different ways. Leaders must provide teams at every level with *differentiated* resources and support.

Importantly, leaders should have initial discussions and make decisions regarding resources for teams at the beginning of the process. Too often, teams receive resources that are not current, or do not fit their specific needs at particular times in the process. In other words, district leaders must model the same intensity and focus on planning for resource allocation for the alignment of the work of teams that they expect of teams as they engage in their work.

Assumption Six: Leaders Monitor and Celebrate the Work of Teams

Aligning and directing the work of teams is not enough. One important way leaders communicate what they truly value is with frequent monitoring of the work of teams and timely and meaningful recognition and celebration along the way (DuFour & Eaker, 1998). When leaders monitor—pay attention—to the *quality of the products* teams produce and the results of each team's improvement efforts, the message is clear: this work is important. The same is true with recognition and celebration. As Tom Peters (1987) writes, "Well-constructed recognition settings provide the single most important opportunity to parade and reinforce the specific kinds of new behaviors one hopes others will emulate" (p. 307).

District leaders who are serious about aligning the work of teams throughout the entire organization should not underestimate the powerful messages they send by monitoring and celebrating the work of each team, as well as the message they send when they monitor and celebrate too infrequently. The traditional annual monitoring of goal attainment and the annual Teacher of the Year banquet are woefully inadequate ways to communicate core values, motivate and inspire others, or simply let people know they are appreciated for doing a difficult and complex job well.

Effective leaders understand that frequent, simple, sincere, and meaningful recognition and appreciation of *improvement* are more effective than the infrequent, large ceremony in which a few are recognized for attaining arbitrary standards. While such ceremonies are important, effective leaders understand that, by themselves, they are inadequate.

The Right Work, the Right Way, for the Right Reasons

So what would it take for district leaders to improve learning districtwide? Could district leaders move beyond reading leadership books and reciting quotes? Could we stop hiding behind budget codes, Excel spreadsheets, compliance reports, and the silos of isolation? Could we stay off our phones long enough to actually engage in the content? Could we operationalize the important research in every school across the district? Could we move beyond giving advice to actually embedding the learning, as well as doing and rehearsing the work? Can we model the leadership behaviors we expect of others in our leadership meetings and in daily practice? Could we move beyond meetings where we fill up the agenda—department by department from human resources to transportation—to meeting with an intentional focus on learning?

If the district office can work as a team that models the concepts and practices of a PLC, system improvement would not be a pipe dream—it would be guaranteed. One would find a guaranteed and viable curriculum in place in all schools in the district. First grade would be first grade across the district; the same essential standards would be in every first-grade classroom. Each would have the same end-of-unit assessments measuring the essential standards unit by unit. Algebra would be algebra in every classroom, and during every period of the day. Essential standards would be the same, as would scope and sequence, and each team would have the same common formative assessments. The only thing that would be different is the art of the teacher, the scaffolding, and the additional time, support, and extensions necessary to ensure learning based on the needs of individual students.

Every educator goes into the profession wanting to be outstanding at his or her craft. Educators want to build relationships with their students and help them learn so they can be college and career ready in order to be successful beyond high school. Educators know that they are the key factor to making a difference in student learning. Leaders at every level must ensure that all teachers on a staff understand that the way they go about their work has a significant impact on student learning—for better or worse.

Simultaneously, leaders must halt the common practice of using other factors such as student home life, socioeconomic status, and lack of motivation as an excuse for poor progress. Yes, these factors can hinder learning and make ensuring student learning more difficult, but great teachers always try to make a difference despite these issues, and they often succeed. District leaders can have a powerful impact on helping every teacher be successful with every student, every day. System enthusiasm and agreement with the concepts and practices of a

PLC won't have much effect on student achievement if the work is not embedded in the day-to-day culture of the district. Collaboratively agreeing isn't the same as collaboratively doing.

So, what would *collaboratively doing* look like if districts were serious about aligning the work of a PLC top to bottom in day-to-day practice? This book seeks to answer this question. It is a call to action. School boards, superintendents, and district office administrators must step up to their responsibility and align the work of teams from the school board to the classroom in order to create a culture of continuous improvement—team by team, task by task, day in and day out, forever.

A Cyclical Process

The work of collaborative teams in a district that functions as a PLC is both a top-down and bottom-up cyclical process. The cycle begins with the school board and superintendent team. Based on an in-depth data analysis, as well as feedback from all teams at other levels, this team develops both short-term and long-term high-priority goals for the district. These goals, along with policies, set a direction and align the work of teams throughout the district. Most importantly, the work of the school board and superintendent team models the work that they expect of others throughout the PLC.

The School Board and Superintendent Team

One of the primary ways organizations communicate what is truly valued is through the behaviors that are modeled, especially by those in top-tier leadership positions. The school board and superintendent team must model the behaviors of an effective high-performing collaborative team. What would lead us to believe that other teams in a district will seek to perform at a higher level more than the team that has the primary responsibility for ensuring high levels of learning for all students throughout the district, as well as building a professional culture that is research-based and data driven?

Through meaningful data-based collaborative goal setting—both short term and long term—the school board and superintendent team has the responsibility for creating a culture of continuous improvement, as well as a culture in which adults find professional success and fulfillment. The phrases "it starts at the top" and "the buck stops here" aptly apply to the school board and superintendent team.

The District Leadership Team

The district leadership team, which is composed of all the district office administrators, principals, assistant principals, teachers on special assignment (TOSAs), and building learning coordinators (BLCs) in the district, is guided by the goals the school board superintendent team has established. This team drills deeper into improving student learning by collaboratively analyzing and sharing student-learning data school by school, grade by grade, and subject by subject, as well as developing additional districtwide SMART goals (strategic and specific, measurable, attainable, results oriented, and time bound; Conzemius & O'Neill, 2013) and improvement initiatives. This team also collaboratively anticipates issues and questions that are likely to arise and the most effective ways to prevent and address these problems and questions. Importantly, when possible, the district-level principal team members practice and rehearse the work that they expect of teacher teams. Thus, they are better equipped to assist teacher teams when the need arises.

The Building Leadership Team

This collaborative team mirrors work of the district-level principal team. Each school-level leader and leaders of individual collaborative teacher teams form this schoolwide leadership team. The school leadership team anticipates issues and questions, shares and analyzes learning data, sets schoolwide SMART goals, and practices and rehearses the work that is expected of teacher teams within the building.

Teacher Collaborative Teams

The school-level teacher collaborative teams comprise teachers who teach at the same grade level or teach the same or similar content. Using the district and school goals as a foundation, teacher teams collaboratively plan units of teaching and learning, clarify what is essential for each student to learn in every unit of instruction, and monitor student learning on a frequent and timely basis using, among other measures, collaboratively developed common formative assessments. They use the results of these assessments to provide students with additional time, support, or extension of their learning, to set team SMART goals, and to reflect on ways to improve their individual and team professional performance.

Importantly, at each level, teams frequently monitor progress and celebrate the improvement of students and adults, both individuals and groups.

Data Flow

In this simultaneous top-down, bottom-up cyclical process, the results flow upward from the teacher teams. Teacher teams share learning data, coupled with feedback and need requests, within the school leadership team. This information is then forwarded to the district leadership team where members analyze data, disaggregate it, and share it with the school board and superintendent team. These data then serve as the primary tool for the school board and superintendent goal-setting process for the next cycle. Goals and direction flow down, while data results, suggestions, input, and needs requests flow up (see figure I.1, page 10).

About This Book

Each chapter in this book focuses on one of these four types of teams and how alignment across a district looks, beginning with the school board and superintendent team in chapter 1 and continuing with the district-level principal team in chapter 2, the school-level principal and grade- or content-leader teams in chapter 3, and the grade-level or content teams in chapter 4. Chapter 5 wraps up the book with some reflection on the benefits of districtwide alignment of the PLC process.

Each chapter provides practices, strategies, and tools for alignment from our experiences in the White River School District in Buckley, Washington.

School Board and Superintendent Team	District Leadership Team	Building Leadership Team	Teacher Collaborative Teams
Composed of the members of the school board and the superintendent	Composed of all the district office administrators, principals, assistant principals, teachers on special assignment, and building learning coordinators within the district	Composed of the principal, assistant principals, and team leaders	Composed of teachers who teach the same grade level, in the same content area, or the same course

School Board and Superintendent Team

- Collaboratively develops operating principles
- Sets direction and focus areas for the district
- Focuses on learning
- Establishes short- and long-term improvement goals
- Aligns policies with the learning mission of the district
- Models research-based and data-driven decision making
- Routinely analyzes improvement data
- Monitors annual learning goals
- Models behaviors expected of others
- Celebrates improvement

District Leadership Team

- Collaboratively develops role definitions and shared commitments
- Develops team norms and accountability protocols
- Focuses on learning
- Holds regular meetings with agendas
- Practices and rehearses the work teacher teams will engage in
- Anticipates questions and issues
- Examines the work of high-performing teacher teams
- Engages in shared learning
- Shares learning data
- Sets individual building commitments based on the work from teacher teams and the building leadership team
- Determines evidence for the next meeting that demonstrates progress toward meeting building commitments
- Monitors results and continuous improvement
- Models behavior expected of others
- Celebrates improvement

Building Leadership Team

- Collaboratively develops role definitions and shared commitments
- Develops team norms and accountability protocols
- Focuses on learning
- Regularly meets using meeting agendas
- Sets improvement goals
- Practices and rehearses the work in which teacher teams will be engaged
- Analyzes student learning, seeks best practice, and shares findings
- Monitors results using a continuous improvement cycle
- Models the behavior expected of others
- Celebrates improvement

Teacher Collaborative Teams

- Develop team norms and accountability protocols
- Focus on learning
- Hold regular meetings with agendas
- Set SMART goals unit by unit
- Analyze student learning, seek best practice, and share findings
- Monitor results using a continuous improvement cycle
- Share results with the building leadership team
- Celebrate improvement

Shares Results and Products With the School Board and Superintendent Team

Shares Results and Products With the District Leadership Team

Shares Results and Products With the Building Leadership Team

Figure I.1: Aligning the work of collaborative teams.

White River School District

White River School District serves a suburban and rural community. Enrollment is just over four thousand students. Thirty percent of students qualify for free and reduced lunch, 15 percent of students qualify for special education services, and approximately 4 percent of students speak English as a second language. The student population is 80.2 percent White, 11.1 percent Hispanic/Latino, 1.3 percent Asian, .6 percent Black/African American, and 5.9 percent two or more races.

The White River School District consists of seven schools from preschool to high school.

- Early Learning Center, PreK and Kindergarten
- Mountain Meadow Elementary, Grades 1–5
- Foothills Elementary, Grades 1–5
- Wilkeson Elementary, Grades 1–5
- Elk Ridge Elementary, PreK–Grade 5
- Glacier Middle School, Grades 6–8
- White River High School, Grades 9–12

Prior to implementation of the PLC at Work process districtwide, there was only one school in White River School District that operated as a PLC. That school, Mountain Meadow Elementary, outperformed the other elementary schools in the district, region, and nearly all elementary schools in Washington State. As a result of that success, district leadership realized that in order for all schools to achieve at high levels, there needed to be a consistent implementation of the PLC process in every school. Districtwide alignment originated with the school board and superintendent with the creation of a clear vision for the work and determining focus areas for schools to implement and monitor. One important focus area was to establish a guaranteed and viable curriculum across the district.

Establishing high-performing collaborative teams became the vehicle to improve learning, and this started with the school board and superintendent team. District office leaders were expected to work collaboratively and lead with the filter of improving learning for all rather than making decisions in isolation based on individual department initiatives. Principals at all levels learned together and implemented PLC concepts and practices in every school in the district. Building leaders created teacher teams at each grade level and in content areas throughout the district. Master schedules were adjusted to give teams time to collaborate and to ensure students received effective interventions at three levels (Tier 1, Tier 2, and Tier 3). The number-one priority and common thread across the district was to live the mission: ensuring high levels of learning for each student, preparing them for success beyond high school. The work surrounding living the mission wasn't one initiative of many initiatives; it was the only district initiative. The White River School District was committed to implementing the PLC process as the vehicle to achieve its mission.

This fourteen-year journey of PLC implementation in White River School District has been sustained by staying the course and by using the four critical questions of learning in a PLC to limit district initiatives. Annually, hundreds of educators from across the United

States visit the White River School District to observe the work of teams and the district systems that have been put in place to support them.

Conclusion

Highly effective PLCs are much more than a group of people working hard at doing the right work. In high-performing PLCs, the work is *structured* and *organized* to flow both up and down in a rational, effective way.

For well over a decade, the White River School district has worked to enhance the effectiveness of data flow and decision-making within the district, and the processes and practices of White River can serve as a valuable case study for others. Not only does this case study focus on the what, but it also looks at the how, including product examples that every district can adapt and use. It is our desire that readers will see this White River case study as a treasure trove of ideas, examples, and products, all of which are geared toward the purpose of helping your district achieve the fundamental purpose of ensuring high levels of learning for every student, every day!

Chapter 1

Starting at the Top: The School Board and Superintendent Team

Effective top-down leadership can have a tremendous effect on the quality of the bottom-up work of school teams. It is unrealistic to think that teams throughout a district will be able to function at a high level if the school board and superintendent team is not functioning at a high level to develop a strong PLC foundation—the district mission, vision, values (shared commitments), and goals; embed a collaborative culture throughout the district; and create a commitment to a data-driven, research-based culture at every level within the district.

District office leaders often shy away from such top-down practices. As Richard DuFour (2007) notes, "Many district leaders are reluctant to champion improvement for fear of being labeled with the epithet 'top-down leader,' the unkindest cut of all" (p. 38). However, as DuFour (2007) contends, "Does professional autonomy extend to the freedom to disregard what is widely considered a best practice in one's field?" (p. 38). Many administrators struggle to expect and require that principals and staff implement best practices.

In White River, we knew we needed to expect and require systemwide adherence to a common mission; a view of what the district was striving to become (vision); collaboratively developed, shared commitments; and targeted, research-based practices. The bottom-up approach—site-based management—was only working at one of nine schools in the district. That school, Mountain Meadow Elementary, was using PLC concepts and practices to improve learning. We began to realize that Mountain Meadow was one of the highest-performing elementary schools in Washington State for that reason, so the district sought to align the PLC process districtwide.

The work of the school board and superintendent team involves educating the board so members understand the concepts, practices, and vocabulary of a PLC at Work—and the expectations and requirements of teams districtwide within the PLC process. We cannot overemphasize the importance of superintendents and district leaders taking time to educate school board members. We contend if the board is educated and has a deep understanding of the why, what, and how involved in advancing the mission of the district, student learning will dramatically increase—not to mention the superintendent will experience longevity in the position.

The school board and superintendent team provides direction and support for districtwide efforts to improve student success. Recall in figure I.1 (page 10) the list of school board and superintendent team tasks.

- Collaboratively develops operating principles
- Sets direction and focus areas for the district
- Establishes short- and long-term improvement goals
- Aligns policies with the learning mission of the district
- Models research-based and data-driven decision making
- Routinely analyzes improvement data
- Monitors annual learning goals
- Models behaviors expected of others
- Celebrates improvement

This team is made up of the superintendent and elected board members. They work closely with the superintendent's cabinet, which is typically assistant superintendents and directors that oversee major arms of the district to include teaching and learning, student support services, equity and achievement, operations, human resources, and business services. These leaders often present information and data relevant to the PLC process in board learning meetings or study sessions. In a small rural district, the superintendent and a single assistant superintendent are likely responsible for some of the previously mentioned roles.

Importantly, the work of the school board and superintendent team is grounded in some basic assumptions. This chapter examines how the members of the school board and superintendent team work to align the work of the PLC districtwide. We use strategies and practices we developed in the White River School District as a template for success.

Focus on the Why: Building Shared Knowledge

Sinek (2009b), in his book *Start With Why: How Great Leaders Inspire Everyone to Take Action*, describes how Martin Luther King Jr. was absolute in his conviction. King knew that change had to happen in America. His clarity of why, his sense of purpose, gave him strength and energy to continue his fight against seemingly insurmountable odds. Sinek (2009b) states, "And that speech was about what he believed, not how they were going to do it. He gave the 'I Have a Dream' speech, not the 'I Have a Plan' speech" (p. 129). In the White River School District, our dream was to have all students learning at high levels. To make this dream a reality, we had to start with the why to build buy-in so we could implement a plan (the PLC process) to reach our dream.

From the school board and the superintendent down to the teacher teams, it is important to start with the why. Typically, educators will not oppose change if they understand why the change is so critically important. As Anthony Muhammad and Luis F. Cruz (2019) point out, "A leader has to create a compelling, fact-based case for change, and then use his or her ability to convince people to make the organizational challenge their personal challenge" (p. 25). In White River School District, we were going to implement PLC at Work concepts and practices. Why? Because, by doing this work, we knew we could improve adult professional practice and student achievement levels at every school, on every team, and in every classroom as measured by multiple indicators to include:

- Grades

- Attendance

- State assessment results

- Student growth data

- Graduation rates

- Enrollment and completion of post-secondary education

- Dual credits earned

- Increased enrollment in AP courses and increased AP courses being offered for successful student completion of a more rigorous and challenging curriculum

- ACT and SAT results

- Positive behavior interventions and support (PBIS) and multitier systems of support (MTSS) data

- Special education data

- Ninety percent K–2 reading goal

- Historically and contemporarily underserved student data (socioeconomic status, race, gender, English learning status, special education status, and so on)

We had a dream that was grounded in students learning at higher levels. To achieve that dream, we had to build shared knowledge and focus work within the school board and superintendent team on actions that, in turn, would build shared knowledge in schools and teacher teams throughout the district. To build shared knowledge at the board level, White River School District required every board member to attend a PLC at Work Institute. (Visit www.solutiontree.com/events/institutes/plc-at-work.html for additional information.) In addition, White River held one board meeting a month that focused on learning about the concepts and practices of a PLC from Mountain Meadow Elementary. During this meeting, invited school grade-level and content-area teams shared their essential standards, common formative assessments, process to analyze data, and how they provided additional time, support, and extensions linked to their formative assessment data. The school board and superintendent team also had the opportunity to view team products. Through these meetings, board members built shared knowledge and a common vocabulary.

Members of the school board and superintendent team also attended collaborative teacher team meetings as observers, watched videos of White River teams doing collaborative work, and engaged in a number of book studies. You would also find board members seated next to staff during districtwide professional development opportunities, included in meetings about the response to intervention process, and involved in the administrative retreat. Hundreds of school leaders visit White River every year to see the work of the district and the collaborative teacher teams. The board president often addresses the site visitors and shares the board role in the PLC journey and how it aligns with the district mission.

Engage in Collaborative Teaming: The Engine That Drives White River

The school board and superintendent team realized that engaging educators to work in collaborative teams was truly the best hope for significantly improving learning across the district. An ADP Research Institute study (Hayes, Chumney, Wright, & Buckingham, 2019) states, "Employee engagement can be complex at both the individual and organizational levels, but one overarching factor emerged from the study: working on a team improves engagement—regardless of demographics, work status, or where someone works" (p. 5).

In the White River School District, the school board and superintendent team aligned the work of teams under the four critical questions of learning that are central to the PLC at Work process (DuFour et al., 2016).

1. **What do we want students to know and be able to do?** Clarifying what all students should learn in every subject, in every grade, in every course, in every unit involves deep collaboration around such topics as essential standards, learning targets, pacing, clarifying the meaning of the standards, clarifying what standards look like in student work, developing proficiency scales, instructional and engagement strategies, and rigor.

2. **How will we know if each student has learned it?** In White River School District, we made a districtwide commitment to focus on the learning of each student, skill by skill. This involves collaboration around benchmark assessments, preassessment, common formative and end-of-unit formative assessments, in-unit quick formative checks for understanding, state assessments, SAT, ACT, and analyzing our results using the TACA process (team analysis of common assessment).

3. **How will we respond if some students do not learn it?** Since we recognized that students learn at different rates and in different ways, we knew each school must develop a systematic plan to provide students with additional time and support if they struggled with some aspect of their learning. This included planning around such topics as differentiated instruction in the classroom and interventions connected to core instruction, which includes additional time and support provided during the school day using response to intervention (RTI) or MTSS, PBIS, social and emotional learning (SEL), and advancement via individual determination (AVID; https://www.avid.org).

4. **How will we extend the learning for students who have demonstrated proficiency?** We recognized that many White River students were under-learning. Furthermore, we wanted to move students beyond proficiency. To extend the learning of students who demonstrate proficiency, each school develops plans around such topics as differentiated instruction, the use of technology,

cooperative teams of students, a more challenging curriculum, and increased rigor.

As DuFour and colleagues (2016) note, in a high-performing PLC, educators work in collaborative teams and take collective responsibility for student learning, rather than working in isolation. Collaborative teams implement a guaranteed and viable curriculum, unit by unit: students receive the same curriculum, regardless of their teacher and within the allotted time. Collaborative teams monitor student learning through an ongoing assessment process that includes frequent team-developed common formative assessments. Educators use the results of common assessments to do the following.

- Improve individual practice.
- Build the team's capacity to achieve its goals.
- Intervene with and extend student learning.

In a PLC, the school provides a systematic process for intervention and extension (DuFour, 2015). DuFour often shared in his keynote addresses that schools don't get to choose the components that they want from the PLC process and disregard the others. If we truly want to improve student learning, we must implement all aspects of the PLC process deeply and well. So, members of the superintendent and school board team knew we had to implement expectations for every team in White River School District.

Emphasize Expectations and Requirements

District office staff often struggle with delivering deliberate messages regarding expectations. However, most educators—actually, most people—are far more productive and satisfied when they know what expectations are and have a clear direction to work toward. As Gene Bottoms and Jon Schmidt-Davis (2010) state:

> Districts must have a long-term plan that includes a vision of effective schools, the intervening steps that schools need to take and the support schools need from the district. The vision and the strategic plan can establish the boundaries in which principals have discretion to operate. They also can enable districts to identify the skills and expertise that district staff, principals and teachers need in order to create effective schools. (p. 25)

Leaders can't be afraid of powerful verbs such as *expect*, *require*, and *support*. They often wonder if it's possible to expect and require and still build positive relationships. District leaders must confidently state (and in our work with school teams, we often ask them to say it aloud): "We're going to expect, require, and support our staff to do the work of ensuring high levels of learning for all of our students by embedding the concepts and practices of the PLC at Work model in our day-to-day work!" In White River, we live by the motto, "Relentless pressure—gracefully applied."

When schools and districts fail to expect and require certain behaviors, they often fall victim to a damaging gap. Robert Eaker and Janel Keating (2008) refer to this as the *expectation-acceptance gap*. This is the significant gap between what district leaders say is expected and what they are willing to accept. There are many places during the PLC journey that can act as parking lots—places where teams get stuck or become complacent. These are bumps in the road that the district and superintendent team can help schools and teams overcome. When teams are doing the right work for the right reasons and at the right time, per district office expectations, they will still hit some bumps. Teams must acknowledge these bumps but not let them become a parking lot. They acknowledge the issue, reflect, take a deep dive back into research, have conversations with the practitioners and one another, and work toward a logical fix. Every single time White River hit a bump, people reflected, made adjustments, and got better. This mindset supports a culture of "We're not there . . . *yet!*"

Direction and Clarity From the Top—Goals

Many school district offices resemble a field of silos; each silo represents an area of responsibility usually connected to a funding source and a budget code—with state or federal compliance attached. For example, there are departments for special education or student support services, Title I, English language learners, Tier 2 and Tier 3 intervention, curriculum and instruction, digital learning, assessment, human resources, and business services. Such silo structures and cultures create a working environment in which district leaders are isolated by compliance, paperwork, meetings, and the next book study. How much of this isolated work actually improves student learning? Districts that operate in this manner do not share responsibility for student learning and do not see the connection between each department and the district mission of ensuring high levels of learning for the students they serve. Rather than coordinating resources and working collectively to guide and support principals, often there are competing priorities that distract from the primary goal. A districtwide PLC seeks to break down these silos, providing direction and clarity from the top of the district down through the individual schools within.

For some leaders, clarity can be scary; if you aren't clear yourself, how can you lead the work effectively? There is a balance when you are a leader of learning. Leaders must have a deep knowledge of the work they are requiring others to do. Nothing can lead a school off the path more quickly than a leader who doesn't exactly understand the why, the what, and the how him- or herself. An important part of successfully leading a school is that all staff do the hard work of learning and understanding best practices and coming to consensus on the why. Once they have done that work, it's easy to expect and require because there is a common understanding regarding why the work is so important.

In the White River School District, there are structures in place that ensure all teams—the district leadership team, building leadership teams, and teacher collaborative teams—receive clear direction and communication from the school board and superintendent team.

The board and superintendent can accomplish this, for example, when they analyze student learning data by grade level, subject, and course. As a result of the data analysis, the school board and superintendent team is able to provide focused direction and goals for each academic year. There's an expectation that individual schools and the teacher collaborative teams within them mirror the same process—analyzing data, setting school SMART goals, establishing team goals, unit by unit, and student goals, target by target (see figure 1.1). It's this process that ensures teams are doing the right work at the right time, for the right reason, and in the right way.

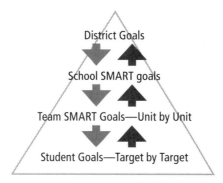

Figure 1.1: District, school, and team goal-setting process.

Loose-Tight Leadership

In a PLC, leaders are tight about what all students must learn—every course, subject, grade, and unit, as agreed on by the teams; leaders are also tight about providing evidence of student learning—student by student, skill by skill. Leaders are tight on best practices for teaching and instructional strategies based on data, while encouraging creativity, individuality, ownership, empowerment, and teachers' professionalism. Leaders cannot expect or require behaviors and actions until they themselves are clear about best practice, expectations, and what the evidence of meeting those expectations would look like. In other words, leaders can't effectively be tight on anything unless they can explain and describe it with great clarity:

> Leaders must realize . . . that the most important element in communicating is congruency between their actions and their words. It is not essential that leaders be eloquent or clever; it is imperative, however, that they demonstrate consistency between what they say and what they do. (DuFour et al., 2016, pp. 14–15)

The school board and superintendent team should expect and require that each department:

- Make student learning the priority and align all practices and procedures to promote student learning
- Measure all major decisions against the probable impact on learning
- Ensure a guaranteed and viable curriculum is in place at every grade level and course (Tier 1 core content)
- Monitor the data and results, and have a "then what?" plan (for Tier 2 and Tier 3 intervention)
- Create systems that house the guaranteed and viable curriculum work (in White River, we use Google Sites for this purpose, which we explore later in chapter 4, page 91) and advance the work of teams. Each teacher collaborative team uses the

same district skeleton unit plan templates that are housed in a Google site. All staff have access to these documents.

These actions will have a positive impact on improving the professional practice of adults and get more students to learn at higher levels, which we define as meeting grade-level expectations and higher. At White River, the process began with setting expectations, continued with developing a written plan, and moved on to scaling the work.

The school board and superintendent team established expectations for teams within the district as well. These included requirements that teams would establish essential learning standards, team-meeting expectations, and a protocol for reviewing common formative assessments.

Process for Establishing SMART Goals

Following are the directions the superintendent provided to each principal and collaborative teacher team leader.

> For your first unit, I want you and your team to identify what learning standard or standards are absolutely essential. Based on the essential standard or standards, what do students have to be able to do? Your team needs to have a conversation about this and come to an agreement.
>
> Next, write down what students must be able to do to be proficient on this standard. Determine "In this unit, students will. . . ." Then, as a team, take time to discuss how you are going to measure what's essential and discuss what proficiency will look like on that assessment. Now it's time to write it down.
>
> As a team, you'll also need to commit to a date to administer the assessment. Then write it down. Your team will then need to determine the percentage of students who will be proficient on this essential standard. Remember to look at how your students performed on this standard last year. You should also look at your benchmark assessments that highlight the percentage of students ready to interact with grade-level standards. Most importantly, establish that percentage you expect to be proficient by the end of the unit by looking at your students—kid by kid. Again, write it down. If there is a percentage of students who aren't proficient on the essential standard, for what portion of the standard will they be proficient? Write that down.
>
> It's also important to note that if students receive additional time and support, the time and support must be aligned with a portion of the standard students must be proficient with in this unit. In short, additional time and support need to be aligned to the SMART goal.
>
> There are also a number of things your team needs to consider. For students who haven't yet mastered the essential standard, when will you next measure their mastery? Write that down. This is a big factor when it comes to closing the achievement gap. If this SMART goal is linked to a grade-level essential standard, students can't leave your class without learning essential standards.
>
> If it's an essential standard that you work on and assess throughout the year, then ask what percentage of students needs to master this standard at this point in the year.

Following are examples of SMART goals at White River.

- **Grade 3:** By the end of unit 2, 71 percent of students (or forty-six students) will be proficient on standard RI.3.2—Determine the main idea of a text; recount the key details and explain how they support the main idea as measured on the unit 2 post-assessment and 3.RI.2 proficiency scale. The remaining 29 percent of students (or nineteen students) will provide key details when the main idea is given or provide the main idea when key details are given, as measured by unit 2 post-assessment and RI.3.2 proficiency scale

- **Algebra:** By the end of the unit, 70 percent of students will demonstrate proficiency on the summative assessment for the following essential skills.
  - Find the slope and y-intercept from a graph, table, and equation.
  - Write the equation of a line in slope-intercept form.
  - Graph the equation of a line.

- *All* students (100 percent) will be able to find the slope and intercept from a graph, table, and equation and write the equation of a line in slope-intercept form.

Expectations for Team Meetings

In White River School District, the superintendent and school board team requires team meetings to be meaningful and effective. We knew this would happen only if people came to each meeting fully prepared. The following is an example of an email from the superintendent that communicates clear expectations for the teacher collaborative team meetings.

> During your Monday weekly collaborative team meeting, come to the table with evidence of student learning. What you bring to the team meetings should reflect what you taught and evidence of what students learned last week. This could be data from a quick formative check for understanding, examples of student work, or data from an end-of-unit assessment.
>
> You need to come to the table prepared to discuss the data and student work and determine next steps. What if you are a secondary teacher and you have 150 students? Do you need to bring 150 examples of student work? No! Bring student work that reflects the common misconceptions related to the essential standard or target that you were teaching and checking on that week. For example, you could bring five to ten papers that represent the kinds of things students are struggling to learn. Likely, the team will focus on identifying instructional strategies that will help these students during core instruction.
>
> If you are using this time to determine who will receive additional time and support, you will need the name of each student and his or her data or student work. The benefit of having students' work at the table is that you can see exactly where the students are struggling. Teams should then move on to discussing the question, What standards and targets will we teach this week?
>
> Your discussion should focus on the targets that you will teach this week related to the essential standard. Your team should also discuss instructional strategies and how to engage students, as well as what resources you will use. The team should also discuss what barriers some students might have to accessing the learning targets for the week. Your

> team should agree on what formative check for understanding, student work, or data you will be bringing to the table next Monday.
>
> That's it! All of this should be part of your work in the team's collaboratively developed unit plan.
>
> Record your conversation in the TACA form (team analysis of common assessment). Every team should use its TACA forms weekly to document formative data and the conversation surrounding the formative data.
>
> Our most effective teams—teams that get results with students—use the TACA process weekly to record the learning journey toward meeting the standard in the unit of instruction. Remember TACA is a protocol and process to talk about your students and their learning.

The following section describes the TACA process using the TACA form.

The TACA Process

Simply developing common formative assessments does little to improve student learning. The key to capturing the power of common formative assessments for teacher teams lies in what teachers do with the results—kid by kid, and skill by skill.

The TACA process (team analysis of a common assessment) is a protocol teams in the White River School District use for reviewing the results of common formative assessments. The TACA process provides a structure to help teams dig into their data, make instructional decisions, and move learning forward. Teams revisit the form multiple times throughout a unit as members look at a variety of common assessments and student work to guide instructional decisions and improve student learning.

Teams take the following steps in the process.

- Enter data.
- Analyze results.
- Make an instructional plan and design support.
- Revisit to revise the plan.

Teams should spend the majority of their time on conversations around designing an instructional plan to support learners who need extra time and support. At White River, teams create the TACA form in Google Sheets so team members can access and use the form at the same time. (At White River, teams find their TACA form in their building's grade-level folder.)

The form includes the following sections.

- **Previous year's TACA:** This TACA contains the unit-by-unit data from each common formative assessment from the previous school year. TACA forms are saved and stored in a Google site. Before teams start planning a unit, they review the TACA from the previous year. This helps to remind the team where students were successful, what instructional strategies and resources worked best, where students struggled, and which skills needed reinforcement.

- **Current year's TACA:** This is the TACA for the current school year. Teams start with a blank TACA at the beginning of each school year.

- **Kid-by-kid data for each individual unit:** Each teacher has a kid-by-kid tab labeled with his or her name to enter data into. Teachers enter a full year of reading and writing on the same form. The kid-by-kid data from individual teachers auto feeds to the team page.

  At White River, each teacher has one (or more) worksheets in a Google Sheets workbook where he or she enters data throughout the year. In ELA (English language arts), for example, there might be one worksheet where a teacher enters student reading data and one where he or she enters student writing data. The worksheets are set up to automatically color code by score as teachers enter data; each score level (1 to 4) is represented with a different color. This provides an "at a glance" view of how the class as a whole performed on an assessment, as well as how an individual student is doing over time. Embedded in the workbook are formulas that count the 1s, 2s, 3s, and 4s and graph them as a percentage of the total students in that class. This allows teacher teams to quickly look at the graph and see which teacher's students struggled and if another teacher's students were very successful. This makes it easy for teams to start the conversation about which teacher instructional strategies might have led the successful students to do well.

- **Postassessment scores:** These scores are linked to each team unit page for easy access.

- **Formative data pages:** Teams can use these pages to capture data for common formative assessments. Make sure the assessments are named the same thing from teacher to teacher, including the standard number and unit number, and are entered in the same column. This is a great spot for tracking SMART goal data.

For each unit, teams address the following questions using the data they entered.

1. What did you learn from revisiting last year's TACA form? (Use at beginning of the unit.)

2. What is the SMART goal for this unit of instruction?

3. What are the power standards (essential standards) taught in this unit of instruction?

4. What parts of the standard or learning targets did our students do well with? Which assessment items?

5. What instructional strategies and lessons supported student success?

6. What misconceptions do we see in student work?

7. What concepts, skills, or reasoning do students need to become proficient?

8. Which students did not master essential standards?

9. How will we provide extra time and support for unlearned skills? What are we going to do about it? How will we check for success?

10. Which students mastered the skills? (See individual teacher tabs for kid-by-kid data.)

11. How will we support learners who need extension? What are we going to do about it?

12. Do we need to tweak or improve the assessment (team-generated and district postassessments)?

Figure 1.2 shows a TACA Google Sheet tab for Reading Class 1 (the reading class for teacher 1). The tabs across the bottom of the sheet show the additional pages of the spreadsheet for Reading Class 2 and Writing Classes 1 and 2. Figure 1.3 (page 26) shows the Formative Reading Class 1 tab of the spreadsheet for entering formative data. After individual teachers enter their data in the formative tab, the sheet automatically creates a team sheet with the collected data from all teachers. This tab (Unit 1 Reading) is shown in figure 1.4 (page 27). Figure 1.5 (page 27) shows the combined teacher data compiled into graph form.

Figure 1.6 (page 28) shows the questions teams use for each unit of study. Many parts of this data protocol will be quick. At the beginning of a unit, the teacher team has opened the previous year's TACA to review where students struggled and make plans to provide added supports *before* the end of the unit. Power or essential standards have already been identified in unit plans, as has the SMART goal for the unit. Teachers have entered their data, kid by kid, and can look at the graphs that summarize how their classes performed, which allows them to quickly answer the questions about where their students did well and where they struggled. The majority of the team collaborative time should then be spent deciding on effective interventions for students who need Tier 2 and Tier 3 supports, as well as extensions for those students who learned it. There is no purpose to administering assessments and collecting data if we do not use it to take purposeful, timely action to improve student learning.

Direction and clarity from the top matter when it comes to the collaboration of teacher teams in a districtwide PLC. As Schmoker (2004) reminds us, "Clarity precedes competence" (p. 85). In addition to the TACA process, the White River School District school board and superintendent team also emphasizes the importance of a positive attitude toward teamwork. Janel Keating and Meagan Rhoades (2019) share the following.

> The most important thing each team member should bring to team meetings is a positive attitude. In the White River School District, there is an expectation that everyone must be a contributing member of his or her team. This means we do more than show up for meetings. It means we must be committed to working interdependently with our colleagues to help all students learn—skill by skill, name by name. We do this not simply because our schools are organized into collaborative teams, but because in this district, we focus on student learning with specificity and fidelity—the belief in what we are doing and that what we are doing is important.
>
> Each of us must be committed to not letting our students or our fellow team members down. White River reflects a culture of mutual accountability. These are our kids, our relatives' kids, our neighbors' kids. What we do in our Monday morning meetings matters—a lot. Remember, it is in these meetings where we do the work that shapes our students' lives, and though often overlooked, the professional lives of all of us. Truly, Monday morning team time reflects White River at its best. As always, thank you for all you do, and equally important, how you do it! (pp. 21–23)

Reading Class 1

SSID*	Special Education	Title	English Learners	Use * to Indicate Support Services		Unit 1			Unit 2			Unit 3		
				Last	First / Teacher	Unit 1 Informational	Unit 1 Literary	Unit 1 Post	Unit 2 Informational	Unit 2 Literary	Unit 2 Post	Unit 3 Informational	Unit 3 Literary	Unit 3 Post

Tabs: Reading Class 1 | Writing Class 1 | Formative Reading Class 1 | Formative Writing Class 1 | Reading Class 2 | Writing Class 2 | Formative Reading Class 2 | Formative Writing Class 2 | Unit 1 Reading | Narrative

*SSID = State Student Identifier

Source: White River School District, 2019. Used with permission.

Figure 1.2: Blank TACA form showing tab for Reading Class 1.

Formative Reading Data Class 1

Use this form as a team to capture data from common formative assessments. Make sure the assessments have the same name from teacher to teacher, including the standard number and unit number, and are entered in the same column. You can rename the column by selecting the cell with the number and renaming it. This is a great spot for tracking SMART goal data.

Use * to Indicate Support Services

SSID*	Special Education	Title	English Learners	Last	First	Teacher	1	2	3	4	5	6	7	8	9	10	11	12	13	14	15	16	17	18	19	20

Tabs: Reading Class 1 | Writing Class 1 | Formative Reading Class 1 | Formative Writing Class 1 | Reading Class 2 | Writing Class 2 | Formative Reading Class 2 | Formative Writing Class 2 | Unit 1 Reading | Narrative

*SSID = State Student Identifier

Source: White River School District, 2019. Used with permission.

Figure 1.3: Blank TACA form showing Reading Class 1 formative tab.

	Unit 1 Informational						Grade Level Total
	Teacher 1 Post	Teacher 2 Post	Teacher 3 Post	Teacher 4 Post			
Intensive							
Approaching							
Meets							
Exceeds							
Total							
Intensive %							
Approaching %							
Meets %							
Exceeds %							

Tabs: Reading Class 1 | Writing Class 1 | Formative Reading Class 1 | Formative Writing Class 1 | Reading Class 2 | Writing Class 2 | Formative Reading Class 2 | Formative Writing Class 2 | Unit 1 Reading | Narrative

Source: White River School District, 2019. Used with permission.

Figure 1.4: Blank TACA form showing unit 1 reading tab.

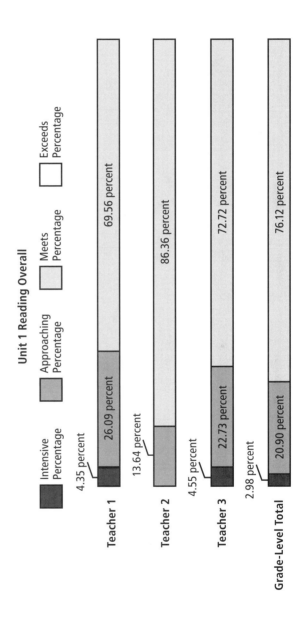

Unit 1 Reading Overall

Legend: Intensive Percentage | Approaching Percentage | Meets Percentage | Exceeds Percentage

Teacher 1: 4.35 percent / 26.09 percent / 69.56 percent
13.64 percent
Teacher 2: 86.36 percent
4.55 percent
Teacher 3: 22.73 percent / 72.72 percent
2.98 percent
Grade-Level Total: 20.90 percent / 76.12 percent

Source: White River School District, 2019. Used with permission.

Figure 1.5: TACA form showing graphed unit 1 reading tab results.

Date:	
School:	
Team:	
	What did you learn from revisiting last year's TACA form? (Use at beginning of the unit.)
What is the SMART goal for this unit of instruction?	
Analyze	What are the power standards (essential standards) for this unit of instruction?
	What parts of the standard or learning targets did our students do well with? Which assessment items?
	What instructional strategies and lessons supported student success?
	What misconceptions do we see in student work?
	What concepts, skills, or reasoning do students need to become proficient?
	Which students did not master essential standards?
Design Support	How will we provide extra time and support for unlearned skills? What are we going to do about it? How will we check for success?
	Which students mastered the skills? (See individual teacher tabs for kid-by-kid data.)
	How will we support the learners in need of extension What are we going to do about it?
	Do we need to tweak or improve the assessment (team-generated and district postassessments)?

Tabs: Reading Class 1 | Writing Class 1 | Formative Reading Class 1 | Formative Writing Class 1 | Reading Class 2 | Writing Class 2 | Formative Reading Class 2 | Formative Writing Class 2 | Unit 1 Reading | Narrative

Source: White River School District, 2019. Used with permission.

Figure 1.6: Blank TACA form showing data protocol questions.

Visit go.SolutionTree.com/PLCbooks to see a completed TACA form for grade 4.

At White River School District, systemwide improvement is not left to the individual teacher collaborative teams, and it's not optional work. Because of the large number of hours being allocated (and the dollars attached to those hours) with the expectation of improving the professional practices of every adult in the system and ultimately improving student learning, there must be a written plan that's operationalized and monitored.

Develop a Written Plan

Everyone who works in schools is busy. But being busy doesn't necessarily mean that educators are accomplishing district goals. We refer to this type of busy as the *illusion of motion*. Essentially, when people are working on things that will have little to no impact on student learning, they are simply accomplishing random tasks. The only way to achieve district mission, vision, and goals is to have a written plan and a system for organization and accountability.

In White River School District, we realized it was not enough to have a sharp focus on student learning, along with a clear vision of the kind of district we hoped to become. We recognized that even having collaboratively developed and shared commitments and goals was not enough. To make our hopes and dreams come alive, we knew we would have to collaboratively develop specific *plans* to ensure action at every level, to get from point A to point B.

From *Hoping* to *Planning*

There is a huge difference between *hoping* for, or even being *committed* to school improvement, and *planning* for improvement. Ultimately, planning is the process through which leaders embed core values in the work at the district, school, and team level. In short, planning institutionalizes what an organization or leader cares about the most. Planning is a way of proclaiming, "This is so important we are going to collaboratively develop a plan to ensure this gets done—on time and with high quality!"

At the most basic level, effective planning is a *collaborative* effort. There is a strong correlation between the quality of collaboration that goes into the planning process and the quality of the plan itself. As Robert Eaker and Debra Sells (2016) point out, "Effective collaboration in, effective plans out!" (p. 116). People who have no, or little, say in the development of plans will have very little, if any, commitment to ensuring the plan succeeds.

Effective planning is more than a mere averaging of opinions. Plans must be relevant and meaningful. Therefore, effective planning is data driven and reflects research-based best practices. And importantly, throughout the entire planning process, effective leaders ensure a constant connection to the why: why each goal is particularly important, and how the goal contributes to the district's mission of high levels of learning for all students, as well as the district's vision of the future. A single initial nod to the why by a leader is never enough; effective leaders frequently connect the planning process back to the why in multiple, clearly articulated ways.

Planning, to a great extent, involves working backward. That is, once planners determine the goal and set the date for achieving the goal, they must identify the major tasks involved in reaching the goal. This way of planning, working backward and identifying major tasks and due dates along with essential activities and completion dates, provides a rational collaborative process that focuses on the right things for the right reasons (Eaker & Sells, 2016).

When planning, once the school board and superintendent team has developed major tasks, activities, and time lines, it is helpful to depict the plan *visually* so that all stakeholders can see what they need to do and when and how the various activities and tasks connect to a larger goal.

The Districtwide Planning Process

Effective planning must be transparent and leaders must monitor it on a frequent and timely basis. One of the most effective ways to make planning transparent and to ensure there is a logical fit for the work educators are undertaking throughout the district is to develop a districtwide calendar. Such calendars, when collaboratively developed by the district leadership team, made available to everyone within the district, and frequently referred to, provide everyone with the same information in a visual format. In short, such calendars take the statement "I didn't know this was due" off the table.

In the White River School District, we stopped assuming our leaders knew exactly what was valued and expected. We developed a district plan that clearly identified the why and spelled out the work and expectations of the district leadership team, building leadership teams, and the teacher collaborative teams.

We wanted to ensure that the work of each team within the district would be aligned to the concepts and practices of the PLC process. We viewed planning as a way of advertising what we cared about the most: student learning. We wanted to communicate to everyone:

> Our mission, our vision, our dream; the shared commitments, goals, and plans will get us there. We are so committed to these things we will develop specific, data-driven plans that reflect best practices throughout the district, in every aspect of what we do.

It was important for us to make sure collaborative planning included certain things. Collaboratively developed written plans should include the major tasks that the school board and superintendent team, district leadership team, and building leadership teams complete along with action steps connected to each task.

Effective plans include thoughtfully developed time lines for completing each task and identifying those who will have primary responsibility for each task, ensuring that those people will complete each task in a high-quality way.

Importantly, we wanted the plans to provide school teams the opportunity to request differentiated support from the district office, since each school has different needs. In addition, we intended for plans to be shared. The products that are developed to align with the district plan are housed in the district Google site, where teacher team members and administrators can frequently view and reference them.

There are many different options for the plan, and no right or wrong choices. It's important that the plan format you use works for your district, starting with the choice of a digital plan, paper plan, or a hybrid.

There are two things that are non-negotiable, however. The first is that the district leadership team will create, support, and monitor the plan. The second is that if the district uses specific tools, especially for calendaring, and a Google site to house the team products, each leader and team needs to commit to using them.

The District Calendar

In *Keeping on Your Feet*, Gene Sharratt (2002) writes of the importance of knowing the difference between the rubber balls and the glass balls in our work: "When rubber balls fall, they bounce back. When glass balls fall, they shatter" (p. 12). From a leadership perspective, the glass balls are the *essential actions* for a leader; without these actions, irreversible damage will occur. The rubber balls, conversely, can be caught on the rebound with little to no harm done. For example, if you file a report late you may get your wrist slapped, but it isn't detrimental to student learning.

At White River, the school board and superintendent team along with the district leadership team spent time identifying all our glass balls: improving and ensuring learning, as well as using the concepts and practices inherent in the PLC concept.

We didn't simply hope that each leader had identified the essential leadership actions tied to learning; we provided them with a calendar that highlighted these actions, month by month, in three areas: (1) the work of the White River School District school board and superintendent team, (2) the work of the district leadership team, and (3) the work of the school building leadership teams. The calendar also includes the purpose and definition of a PLC as shown in figure 1.7 (page 32). However, leaders can add to the essentials based on the student learning needs in their schools. These drive how the school board and superintendent team members allocate our time and the collaborative work that will occur during our leadership meetings (see figures 1.8, 1.9, 1.10, and 1.11, pages 33–40).

It is easy for district leaders to become overwhelmed by day-to-day minutiae. They are so busy putting out the little fires that start all around them that they don't have time to tend to the fireplace that keeps the building warm, stoking the embers of student learning. These overwhelmed leaders have not planned an organized system. In White River School District, the school board and superintendent team have implemented a districtwide planner to help leaders manage their time.

White River School District School Board and Superintendent Team

Purpose of the White River School District School Board and Superintendent Team

To create a common and concise framework to effectively implement PLC concepts and practices with fidelity across the White River School District.

Areas White River School District Is Trying to Improve by Implementing the PLC Process

To improve adult professional practice and student achievement levels at every school, on every team, and in every classroom as measured by multiple indicators to include:

- Grades
- Attendance
- State assessment results
- Graduation rates
- AP scores and results
- ACT and SAT results
- Dual enrollment earned
- Ninety percent K–2 reading goal
- Enrollment in or completion of post-secondary education

Definition of a PLC

A professional learning community (PLC) is "an ongoing process in which educators work collaboratively in recurring cycles of collective inquiry and action research to achieve better results for students they serve" (DuFour et al., 2016, p. 10).

Rationale for PLC Work

Research has shown the PLC concept and related practices, if implemented fully and with fidelity, to be an effective approach for improving student learning.

Source: White River School District, 2019. Used with permission.

Figure 1.7: Purpose and definition page of district PLC planning tool.

The District Planner

Too often each scheduled event during the year arrives as a surprise to leaders, creating a flurry of emergency actions they and others must take. Let's be honest—most events in a school district are not actually a surprise; they are what we call *Groundhog Day events*. From board meetings to the administrative retreat to district data meetings, each event arrives at about the same time of the year, year after year. Yet for many leaders, these events still sneak up on them, leading to a rush to plan and prepare. In fact, the best time to plan for these recurring events is right after the event takes place. It gives an opportunity to reflect on what went well and what pieces need to be adjusted.

There is no right or wrong system of organization, although we advocate that you incorporate a paper system, at least in part. According to Laura Deutsch (2017) in *Psychology Today*, "Writing by hand connects you with the words and allows your brain to focus on them, understand them and learn from them." When you take a little time in the morning to sit down, look at your schedule, clarify what the mission-aligned priorities are, and think about who you need to connect with during the day and why, your day will be more productive and focused on student learning. It doesn't prevent fires, but it keeps you from spending one minute more on them than you need to, because you are clear about the more important things that are awaiting your time.

Work of the White River School District School Board and Superintendent Team				
What are the fundamental tasks for the White River School Board and Superintendent Team?				
Tasks	Actions	Responsibility*	Time Line*	Cost*
1	Establish the why: examine student learning data, attendance, dropout data, historically and contemporarily underserved student data, and special education data	Paint a data portrait of the White River School District (assessment department creation). See *Learning by Doing* (DuFour et al., 2016; August 1).			
		Paint a data portrait of each school (assessment department creation). See *Learning by Doing* (DuFour et al., 2016; August opening day with staff).			
2	Build shared knowledge, provide common training, and communicate extensively surrounding what a PLC is and how it works with an emphasis on why we are doing this work.	Deliver an ongoing message of why PLCs and a focus on learning (Superintendent Keating).			
		Share (or give refresher about) district plan for implementing PLCs.			
		Establish clear direction for how to use the time carved out for PLC work, staff meetings, and professional development. Describe what it is and the responsibilities for all levels (layers of accountability). Provide the monthly planning tool and team planner.			
		Provide examples of the work of a team.			
3	Establish and provide training surrounding common PLC vocabulary (assessment language and literacy, essential standards, and so on).	Provide a common PLC message to all staff in May and August (at the end of school and during the back-to-school event).			
		Provide summer principal and assistant principal professional development.			
		Establish and provide a specialized academy focused on leading the work of improving learning in the district for principals and team leaders.			
		Reframe the monthly principal's meetings with a solid focus on learning using the research from *Raising the Bar and Closing the Gap* (DuFour, DuFour, Eaker, & Karhanek, 2010).			
		Determine school sites that will need ongoing leadership support to operationalize the PLC process.			
		Develop a monthly planning calendar for school and team use (loose-tight).			
4	Review all policies, practices, and procedures to align with a mission of ensuring high levels of learning for all students (superintendent).				

Figure 1.8: District task page of the district PLC planning tool.

continued →

Tasks	Actions	Responsibility*	Time Line*	Cost*
5	Establish and communicate clear expectations and accountability for this work for principals and staff (superintendent).	Reframe principals' meetings and revisit principal and teacher evaluations to include the work of implementing the PLC process.			
6	Develop commitment statements at each level within the district. The school board and superintendent team, district leadership team, building leadership team, and teacher collaborative teams should answer the question, What commitments do we need to make to improve student learning?				
7	Establish sacred PLC time for each team. This means no department meetings, staff meetings, or district trainings during this time.	Clarify and communicate clear directions on how to use the time carved out for PLC work, staff meetings, and professional development. Clarify a process for monitoring the work of teams using a monthly planning tool.			
8	Set meaningful SMART goals unit by unit to support overarching school and district SMART goals.	Establish and provide training on the purpose of SMART goals, writing SMART goals, and monitoring SMART goals at the district, school, and team level.			
9	Establish and use a balanced assessment process to inform and improve professional practice and better meet the needs of individual students.	District content specialist works with districtwide content teams to create pre– and post–common formative assessments, unit by unit; works with teams to understand the purpose of quick checks for understanding and responsive assessment; and provides training on how best to analyze data. Specialist establishes and delivers professional development on the purpose of all assessment processes.			
10	Establish time for students to receive extra support and extensions that are timely and layered.	Implement an additional time and support period at every school, build additional time and support into core instruction, and build intervention and extension opportunities into each unit plan.			

11	Widely communicate with all stakeholders, in multiple ways, the district's mission, as well as a vision of improved student learning at every school, in every classroom, and with every student.	Communicate Superintendent Keating's and the governing board's messages linked to each school website. Be transparent about the school data.		
12	Establish a district PLC evaluation process. (See example in *Every School, Every Team, Every Classroom* [Eaker & Keating, 2012].)	Design a PLC survey to examine student achievement data and collect anecdotal data at each school site. Report progress to all stakeholders.		
13	Attend a PLC Institute.	District office board members, principals, assistant principals, and building learning coordinator attend Seattle PLC Institute.		
14	Establish position description, selection process, and stipend for building learning coordinator and team leader positions.	Craft position description, selection process, and stipend amount for building learning coordinator and team leader positions.		

*The team fills in these columns as it reviews the plan.

Source: *White River School District, 2019. Used with permission.*

> **Work of the District Leadership Team**
>
> **Definition of Collaboration**
>
> Collaboration in a PLC is a systematic process in which educators work interdependently to analyze and impact professional practice in order to improve their individual and collective results. The PLC process requires educators to work collaboratively rather than in isolation and to take collective responsibility for student learning. The collaborative team must replace the isolated classroom as the fundamental structure of the school. Collaborative teams are the engines that drive the organization's efforts to achieve its mission of high levels of learning for all students.
>
> **Rationale for Collaboration**
>
> - It is research based.
> - It is relevant to our work as professionals.
> - It is a collective effort to change perception from "I can't" to "We can" (pool our energy and experience and share the load).
> - It allows us to work together to ensure a guaranteed and viable curriculum across the district.
> - It is the best structure for adult learning that's relevant, job embedded, collective, ongoing, and specifically linked to school and team goals.

Source: White River School District, 2019. Used with permission.

Figure 1.9: Purpose and definition page of district calendar.

School leaders begin each day with a limited amount of time and energy. Every time a leader makes a decision, it depletes energy from that store, lessening what we have left for the rest of the day. Every minute spent on something unimportant is a minute away from the core mission of learning for all. Leaders are used to talking about how important seat time is in the classroom, but we don't typically spend a lot of time talking about adult learning. A laser-like focus on learning means that *adult time and energy* are spent on the things that increase learning.

Having clarity regarding mission, tasks, and roles streamlines the work. When a leader must make every decision, or answer every question on the fly, staff members rely more and more on the leader to provide that decision or answer. When it's extremely clear to everyone what the mission is, when every decision and every answer aligns with the mission, staff become confident about what the decision or answer will be. Clarity of roles—from teacher, to team leader, to school leadership team—means that staff know exactly who to go to for a specific reason, and if they go to the wrong person, they can be easily directed back to the person who owns that role. Think about the times when you have been forwarded from person to person before you get an answer to a question; not only is your time wasted, but every person you spoke to who didn't have the answer was taken away from a task. The written planning processes outlined in this section align the work of those in the district so educators at all levels understand the tasks they must tackle and who to go to when a need arises. *The Leading PLCs at Work® Districtwide Plan Book* (Eaker, Hagadone, Keating, & Rhoades, 2021)—a companion to this book—is a tool to assist district leaders and school administrators in implementing the concepts and practices of a PLC. An excerpt from the plan book appears in figure 1.12 (page 41). (Visit **SolutionTree.com** to order your own copy of the *Leading PLCs at Work® Districtwide Plan Book*.)

PLC Tasks for the District Office			
Tasks	**Actions**	**Responsibility**	**Time Line**
1	Deliver common message on PLC regarding the work of a team.	Share ongoing written communication and video messages from Superintendent Keating to include the following.		
		• Importance of the work and expectations for each principal, teacher, and team within and across campuses		
		• Examples of the work of a team		
		• The additional time and compensation provided to do PLC-related work beyond one hour per week (time provided) with equity across campuses		
		• Where you get help to include neutral help (clarified in Superintendent Keating's messages)		
		• Definition of tight and loose in the district regarding all aspects of PLC work		
2	Provide leadership training that will support the work of a team for the principals, assistant principals, TOSA, instructional coaches, and team leaders.	Establish and deliver a principal, assistant principal, and professional development specialist summer academy focused on leading the work of improving learning in the district.		
		Establish and deliver common team leader, instructional coach, and TOSA training on each campus.		
		Create specific team leader and building leadership coordinator position descriptions.		
		Create an accountability plan for the principal and team leader.		
		Reframe the purpose and work of the monthly principal's meeting to include the assistant principals and a teacher from each campus.		
		Facilitate administrative meetings that model the PLC process: look at data, analyze data, and so on.		
		Determine school sites that will need ongoing leadership team support to operationalize the PLC process.		

continued ➡

Figure 1.10: PLC tasks for the district office on the district PLC planning tool.

Tasks	Actions	Responsibility	Time Line
3	Determine essential standards by grade level and course to include career and technical education courses.		
4	Develop a skeleton unit plan by grade level and by course.	Align the work of the district curriculum office to support the work of the principal and team. (This is the difference between support and compliance.) Assistant superintendent for teaching and learning, curriculum and assessment department, technology department, TOSAs, instructional coaches, and effective staff per grade level and content area will join together to create the following unit by unit.		
5	Create end-of-unit common formative assessments by grade level and course.	• Identify essential standards.		
6	Clarify the purpose and role of the common formative assessment and check for understanding.	• Create unit plans. • Create common formative end-of-unit assessments with feedback protocol (feedback loop).		
7	Communicate clear expectations for curriculum department roles, team use of unit plans and assessments, timely feedback, and reflection to help teams continuously improve.	• Determine additional time, support, and extensions.		
8	Define the feedback loop between the school teams and the district office.			
9	Clarify the purpose and expectations surrounding the unit plans and common assessments aligned to the unit plans.			
10	Provide a protocol and tool from the district to gather data, unit by unit and team by team. These data will be organized and housed in a site that is transparent to teams across the district.	Establish district location or site to house all the work (rights, naming protocols, and so on). Train teams to use data tool.		
11	Create protocols to address conflict and resisters.	Create the common expectations of every team member and protocols for conflict and resisters.		
12	Provide resources to do the work.	Purchase *Learning by Doing* (3rd ed.; DuFour et al., 2016); *Concise Answers to Frequently Asked Questions About Professional Learning Communities at Work* (Mattos, DuFour, DuFour, Eaker, & Many, 2016), and so on.		

Source: White River School District, 2019. Used with permission.

PLC Tasks in the Schools				
School Tasks		Actions	Responsibility	Time Line
1	Organize school staff into meaningful teams.	Assign teachers to no more than two teams.		
		Establish times for teams to meet weekly; one hour should be the standard.		
		Provide a monthly planning calendar that can also be used as an agenda.		
		Select building leadership coordinator and collaborative team leaders.		
2	Make a plan for singletons.	Link singleton teachers with at least one other singleton teacher from another school and establish meeting time and location (virtual or in person).		
3	Establish norms and accountability protocols based on the work of teams.	Reference chapter on norms in *Learning by Doing* (DuFour et al., 2016; pp. 211–232).		
		Share the work related to the four critical questions of a PLC and repeating process in a cycle of inquiry.		
		Read blog post "Do We Have Team Norms or 'Nice to Knows'?" (Williams, 2010).		
		Each team writes norms and accountability protocols.		
4	Define *consensus*.	Every staff member reads and discusses chapter 9 in *Learning by Doing* (DuFour et al., 2016) annually.		
5	Implement a guaranteed and viable curriculum. • Write unit plans. • Clarify standards and learning targets. • Create pacing guides. • Identify evidence of mastery in student work per standards and targets. • Design instruction, sharing instructional strategies, best practice, and engagement strategies (loose).	Implement team by team or course by course. • Write and refine unit plans. • Clarify standards and learning targets. • Use pacing guides. • Identify evidence of mastery in student work as related to standards and targets. • Design instruction and share instructional strategies, best practices, and engagement strategies (loose).		

continued →

Figure 1.11: PLC tasks for the school on the district calendar.

School Tasks		Actions	Responsibility	Time Line
6	Implement a balanced assessment process, including ongoing formative assessment and frequent team- and district-developed common assessments. Provide benchmark assessment system as an outside indicator of student learning. Use common assessment data to determine effectiveness of individual and collective teaching practices and student learning; identify students in need of additional time, support, and extension. Ensure intervention process is fluid and flexible, timely, and directive. Create a defined time period during the school day for intervention and extension.	Implement a balanced assessment process to include ongoing formative assessment in the classroom and frequent team- or district-developed common assessments. Provide benchmark assessment system as an outside indicator of student learning. Use common assessment data to determine effectiveness of individual and collective teaching practices and student learning and identify students in need of additional time, support, and extensions. Ensure intervention process is fluid and flexible, timely, and directive. • Use defined period during the school day for intervention (advisory period) and extensions.		
7	Design and deliver differentiated professional development related to the concepts and practices of a PLC based on the needs of the team.	Design and deliver differentiated professional development related to the concepts and practices of a PLC based on the needs of the team.		
8	Identify and use protocols for examining evidence of student learning (data).	Train teams to analyze data and use district protocols.		
9	Craft collective commitments.	Read "Shift in School Culture" (Eaker & Keating, 2008) and write collective commitments, team by team.		
10	Review protocols to address conflict and resisters.	Follow protocol created by Superintendent Keating and team.		

Source: White River School District, 2018. Used with permission.

SEPTEMBER PLC WORK

- Review scope and sequence of essential standards by grade level and content area.
- Set teacher observation schedule to align with essential standards in content areas and grade levels.
- Review staff expectations surrounding collaboration.
- Visit collaborative meetings to observe evidence of the following.
  - Norms, accountability protocols, and collective commitments
  - Essential standards and learning targets
  - Data or student work at the team table
  - Discussion surrounding where students did well and instructional strategies that helped students
  - Discussion surrounding additional time, support, and extensions
  - Discussion surrounding the next targets and instructional strategies and formative assessment
- Review products from weekly collaborative meeting with administrative team, instructional coaches, and teachers on special assignment.
- Analyze benchmark assessment results in English language arts and mathematics.
- Observe core instruction (Tier 1).
- Observe Tier 2 intervention. Is there a direct connection to core instruction (Tier 1)?
- Observe Tier 3 intervention. What universal skills are being taught using a researched-based curriculum? Review the progress-monitoring data. Reminder the following: Tier 3 students receive all three tiers of instruction.
- Craft school-improvement plan.
- Plan team learning celebration. Celebrate the things you value for students and staff.
- Hold leadership team meeting.
- Determine learning focus of the staff meeting aligned with the district leadership team meeting and the building leadership team meeting held last month, and the school improvement plan.
- Analyze data from the next end-of-unit assessment and schedule vertical articulation team meetings based on data.
- Provide data report to the school board.
- Plan for schoolwide social-emotional learning focus.

NOTES

September Management Work

- [ ] Host back to school night and curriculum night.
- [ ] Check in with new staff members.
- [ ] Conduct benchmark testing.
- [ ] Hold a staff meeting.
- [ ] Hold a PTA or PTO meeting.
- [ ] Conduct bus safety drills.
- [ ] Review parent drop-off and pick-up information.
- [ ] Review emergency procedures and schedule drills.
- [ ] Plan for ongoing events.
  - Assemblies to include student achievement
  - Student of the month awards (school, Rotary, Kiwanis, and so on)
  - Field trips
- [ ] Meet with substitute teachers.
- [ ] Establish student-growth goals.

September Building Work

- [ ]
- [ ]
- [ ]
- [ ]
- [ ]
- [ ]
- [ ]
- [ ]

NOTES

DATE _____

MONDAY

TUESDAY

WEDNESDAY

THURSDAY

FRIDAY

COMPLETE TASK LIST
- [ ]
- [ ]
- [ ]
- [ ]
- [ ]
- [ ]
- [ ]
- [ ]
- [ ]
- [ ]
- [ ]
- [ ]

NOTES

MUST-DO LIST

TEN-MINUTE TASKS

Phone Calls

Emails

Classrooms Check Ins

Feedback and Follow Up

Celebrations of Success

Positive Note

Positive Parent Connections

Self-Care Plan

Big Projects Ongoing or Upcoming

Source: Eaker, Hegadone, Keating, & Rhoades, 2021.

Figure 1.12: White River School districtwide plan book excerpt.

Scale the Work

Every year the White River School District welcomes hundreds of visitors who travel to the district to observe the work of grade-level and content teams. They also come to see the districtwide systems in place to support teamwork. They are able to witness the guaranteed and viable curriculum in every school across the district. They want to learn how we've managed to make third-grade learning consistent across the district. This includes the same essential standards, the same pacing, and the same common formative end-of-unit assessments.

They want to see how our teams analyze their data and student work and what it looks like to provide additional time, support, and extension during the school day, at every level, and in every school. These visitors travel from across Washington State, Oregon, Arizona, and Montana—just to name a few. They have many job titles in districts of every size. During site visits to White River, we often hear the following comment: "You can implement the concepts and practices of a PLC because your district is larger than ours." Visitors from larger districts frequently will comment, "You can implement PLC concepts and practices because your district is small." The superintendent simply responds, "We can implement these concepts and practices because we have the will to do it!" In addition, we know our compelling why. District size shouldn't be more important than research and best practice. DuFour and Marzano (2011) ask, "Will you focus on what is within your sphere of influence and dedicate yourself to making it better, or will you assign both blame for your current reality and responsibility for improving to others?" (p. 208).

Every district is unique, but the basic structure is the same, whether you are a K–12, K–8, or 9–12 district and whether you are large or small. The mission is the same: improving student learning and preparing students for success beyond high school. District size simply means leaders will need to scale the work differently.

From kindergarten upward, each skill and each standard that students reach is a rung in the ladder that gets them to graduation. Before scaling the work in each region or feeder pattern, the assistant superintendents must know the PLC work deeply and well. In a smaller district, students from Elementary A (or Elementary A and B) all go to one middle school and one high school. In a larger district you might have all students from Elementary A through D attending Middle School and High School A, while Elementary E through I attend Middle School and High School B. They must operate as a collaborative team with the same expectations they have of other teams in the district.

For example, every district must have a districtwide guaranteed and viable curriculum. A student's address should not determine what he or she is expected to learn. When leaders and teams guarantee *all* students will learn the collaboratively agreed-on essential standards, they are ensuring that students will be prepared in the same way across the district for the next grade level or course. They can't make this guarantee if each school selects its own essential standards based solely on the perceived needs of their students. In order to ensure a guaranteed and viable curriculum, assistant superintendents must agree on a process and a common protocol that principals and staff in all schools will use. They ask each collaborative team to engage in this discussion and, again, use a common protocol to guide their work surrounding selecting essential standards. Chris Jakicic (2017) recommends using Larry Ainsworth's (2004) book *Power Standards*, in which he lays out a step-by-step guide for determining essential standards:

1. Ainsworth recommends that teams start by having each teacher reflect on which standards he or she believes best represent the most important standards.

2. Once they have completed this process, the team begins to build consensus on which standards they can agree are the most important. He suggests that the essential standards should represent approximately one-third of their curriculum (Ainsworth, 2010).

3. After they've completed this work, the next step is to review any standards documents or test blueprints that provide additional information about expectations for student learning. When teachers start to do this work, they are definitely "learning together" about their standards.

4. The last step in this process is for teams to do a vertical alignment from one grade level to the next or one course to the next. Teachers examine the draft list of essential standards to see how well they line up. They answer the question, "If a student goes through our school and only learns these standards, will he or she be prepared for the next grade level?" They look for repetition or gaps in learning. They examine the grade level before theirs to make sure students will have the necessary prerequisite skills, and the grade level after theirs to make sure their students will be prepared for the rigor expected.

Once this process takes place at every school, district leaders ask that every team submit its grade-level essential standards to the district. A district office team, which includes the assistant superintendents, principals, and teachers from grade-level teams in each area or region, then engage in a review of the essential standards. It is likely that patterns will emerge. The district team then creates a list of *common* essential standards that emerge from the school teams. They also create a list of outliers: essential standards that emerge from some teams but not all teams.

The district leadership team sends the list of agreed-on essential standards and outliers to the building teacher collaborative teams for feedback. We refer to this as an accordion process. The key to this process is input and ownership by all teams in the district. The teams have been engaged and part of the process for determining essential standards. Using this process, district leaders can guarantee that each elementary school is commonly preparing its students for middle school, each middle school is commonly preparing its students for high school, and every course in the high school will have a common set of essential standards. Algebra will be algebra in every high school across the district. What is different at each school are the instructional strategies teachers use and the way the school uses additional time, support, and extensions to help all students meet essential standards. This is an example of doing the work of a PLC districtwide.

Mastering foundational work is the key to enhancing student success. Mike Mattos (2019) says, "If you can reasonably expect that a student will live on their own at some point in their life, then you should expect that they will learn the essential or power standards at each grade."

We know that if a student leaves kindergarten and hasn't mastered the essential standards there, he or she will struggle in first grade. If the student's first-grade teacher doesn't manage to teach him or her the kindergarten essential standards *as well as* the first-grade essential standards, the student will struggle even more in second grade. We know students come to kindergarten with many readiness-to-learn levels. And what data tell us is that if we don't close the gap that year, the struggle won't get easier.

Districts cannot afford to improve schools one school at a time; they must engage in improvement work districtwide—every school and every team.

Consider the following example of Chino Valley Unified School District in Chino Valley, California, a district that educates nearly 32,000 students.

> Our journey into understanding and developing a districtwide PLC in Chino Valley Unified School District first began in 2008. Led through a district initiative, all thirty-five schools in the district brought their guiding coalitions together to learn how collaborative teams could rally around the right work to improve student learning outcomes. With a great prevailing sense of hope and excitement, all teams were committed to the vision of learning for all. As quickly as the teams were fired up, however, the flames quickly fizzled, leaving individual teams to figure out how to improve student learning.
>
> Fast forward to 2016, as assistant superintendent of human resources and associate superintendent, I, along with the deputy superintendent who is now the superintendent, received a request from the teachers' association to abandon the PLC process. The staff did not embrace the built-in weekly time for team collaboration along with other PLC practices and processes. Teams were being asked to collaborate, and I believe they were doing everything they knew how to do, yet they did not see the value of the collaborative work. Some schools worked hard at using the four critical questions of a PLC to work through collaboration; other schools used this dedicated time for administrative staff meetings, extended lunch periods for staff, baby showers, lesson planning, and so on. As a district, we failed to create buy-in and excitement with staff and build the necessary knowledge so teams could apply what they learned to do the work of a PLC. It was not surprising that teachers were asking to use time set aside for collaborative teams for the wrong work, or activities not related to work at all.
>
> The Board of Education requested that Chino Valley allow teacher teams to use at least one of their built-in collaboration days during the month

for individual preparation time. A year passed with teachers having dedicated, banked time to individually prepare to ensure learning for all. We knew we were at a breaking point. With the focus on the what and the how of professional learning communities, we failed to build a collective understanding on the why behind this work. No wonder when the going got rough through our inconsistently consistent practices across the district, the arrival of the Common Core standards, and 21st century learning, we wanted to abandon team collaboration because it was not a valuable use of our time.

With an urgency to calibrate our understanding of PLC and rejuvenate our fire for what we could do to elevate student achievement, district management with the teacher association leadership attended a PLC summit to build a shared understanding of professional learning communities. We agreed that professional learning communities were what we needed if we wanted to recommit to the elevated learning outcomes for every student. We agreed that it was our fundamental responsibility to actualize this purpose, and it was within our control to help all students learn at higher levels. We understood the why behind this important work.

The teachers' association and the district recommitted to the rejuvenation of professional learning communities and agreed that we are the ones who can control what we do for our students. Since our time at the PLC summit, 100 percent of our teachers have gone through trainings to build their capacity to participate and grow in a professional learning community, every school site has expanded their PLC guiding coalition members, and the central office has worked through a top-down, bottom-up approach in building our collective capacity and accountability. Through collaboration with our teachers' association, we have used what we have coined as our "yellow sheet" to lay out what we are going to be tight about and loose about in our development with PLCs.

In only one short year, our student achievement data reflect our recommitment to the hard work. We continue to learn by doing while ensuring that we revisit the why behind this work. We consistently communicate what we value, spend dedicated time on the work we value, reflect and provide feedback to our site administrators and their teams on the work that we value. Interestingly, at one of our board meetings, a board member asked what we had done with our PLC work because she had not heard any complaints this year. It is when we lead with the why that we can get through the what and the how when things get complex and hard. For our students, we know this recommitment to professional learning communities is a journey that was worth taking again! (G. Park, personal communication, October 11, 2019)

Chino Valley was recognized as a Positive Outlier District for its achievement with underrepresented student groups as compared to the rest of the state of California for African American and Hispanic students (Podolsky, Darling-Hammond, Doss, & Reardon, 2019). Figure 1.13 is Chino Valley's Collaborative Team Actions Simplified tool that the school used to achieve its results.

Conclusion

An effective school board and superintendent team can have a transformational impact on the quality of work in every team across the district, measuring all major decisions against the probable impact on student learning. In order to be effective, the school board needs to be well versed in the concepts and practices of a PLC. Done well, their work will make student learning the priority and align all practices and procedures to promote student learning. Driven by a well-developed written plan, they exhibit urgency around student achievement data and are able to answer the questions, Are students learning, and how do we know?

Collaborative Team Action (Bold indicates actions that are tight for the school year.)	PLC Critical Questions			
	1. What do we want students to know and be able to do?	2. How will we know if they have learned it?	3. What will we do if they are not learning it?	4. What will we do when they have learned it?
Develop team norms that are beyond general professional courtesies.				
Write a SMART goal and routinely monitor progress toward meeting it.				
Deconstruct the ten to twelve essential standards into learning targets.				
Before Instruction of the Unit				
1. **Identify and calibrate the team's understanding of the essential standards that correspond with the upcoming unit.** • **What students must know and be able to do to be proficient with the essential standards (success criteria)** • **The student friendly, "I can" statements for the essential standards**	X			
2. **Determine which essential standards and learning targets require a common formative assessment (CFA) during the unit for student and team feedback. Create CFA or CFAs (two versions) with administration and scoring agreements.**	X	X		
3. Create end-of-unit assessment.		X		
4. **Tentatively plan for the number of days allocated for teaching the unit.**	X			
During Instruction of the Unit				
5. **Clarify for students the essential standards;** have students reflect on their learning.	X	X		
6. Analyze CFA data using a data protocol, by student and learning target.		X		
7. Identify a team plan to address the results of the CFA.			X	X
8. **Collectively respond with intervention and extension for the learning target or targets with Tier I and Tier 2 instruction.**			X	X
After Instruction of the Complete Unit				
9. Analyze end-of-unit assessment and determine next steps for Tier 1 and Tier 2 instruction.		X	X	X
10. Have students reflect and set continued learning goals.	X		X	

Source: Chino Valley High School, 2019–2020. Used with permission.

Figure 1.13: Chino Valley's Collaborative Team Actions Simplified in a PLC at Work tool.

Chapter 2

Setting the Stage: District Leadership Team

The focus of this chapter is transforming the traditional district office administrative team into a district leadership team. A traditional district office team consists of the superintendent, assistant superintendent, and the directors of each department. In a traditional school district, building principals are often invited to a scheduled meeting to receive "nuts and bolts" information for their schools. Information typically flows one way—from the district office to the building level—without any bottom-up input from individual building principals. While student learning is an assumed priority, there may be no explicit conversations regarding consistency in this priority from building to building; no one is asking the questions, "Are our students learning, and how do we know?"

In the White River School District, this team consists of the following members of the district office: the superintendent, deputy superintendent, director of finance, director of human resources, director of digital learning services, director of business and operations, executive director of equity and student support services, student support services director, district assessment coordinator, and teachers on special assignment (TOSAs). From the individual schools, teams include the principal, assistant principal, dean of students, career and technical education (CTE) director, and building learning coordinators (BLCs).

To become a learning-focused district, we added building principals and building learning coordinators to the traditionally structured office administrator team. While the school board and superintendent team described in the previous chapter provides direction and support for district-wide efforts to improve student success, it is the role of the district leadership team to develop the practices and procedures that will make the district vision a reality.

At White River, we planned for the district leadership team to be the primary vehicle for getting everyone headed in the same direction with PLC implementation and to ensure improved learning for both students and adults. As we discussed in chapter 1, in traditional districts, educators often operate as independent silos, paying attention to only the immediate needs in their department or school. In a learning-first district, the goal of improving learning for all students in the district is every employee's priority.

Unfortunately, good intentions do not create a learning-first culture. Specific structures, policies, and procedures must be embedded into the work, day in and day out. The message must always be, "This is how we do things here!" This chapter will highlight how White River's district leadership team focuses on collaboration, direction, and support for principals and their teams based on the work required to answer the four critical questions of a PLC. It will drill deeply into the work of this team and the role of the building principal. We will share how the district leadership team at White River moved from holding traditional "nuts and bolts" meetings to meetings in which district leaders, principals, and building learning coordinators practice and rehearse the work, anticipate issues and questions, and share learning data from each school-level principal and grade-level or content team leaders, as well as the school grade-level or content teams within each school.

At White River, we realized the success of each school's teacher collaborative teams depends on the skill and knowledge of the building principal.

We moved to a focus on structural and cultural changes around the role of the building principal. We talked about how to support principals in their efforts to embed the concepts and practices of the PLC at Work process within each school in order to enhance student learning. We realized that in order to improve the effectiveness of each principal, we would have to ensure that principals worked together as part of a high-performing collaborative team.

DuFour (2015) reminds us that the role of the principal "is daunting but doable. . . . A coordinated team approach between the central office and building principal increases the likelihood of success in this most challenging of jobs" (p. 247). We learned that to enhance and support principal leadership, we had to provide clarity regarding the work and expectations and create layers of leadership throughout the system. As DuFour (2007) writes:

> One of the most essential responsibilities of leadership is clarity—clarity regarding the fundamental purpose of the organization, the future it must create to better fulfill that purpose, the highest leverage strategies for creating the future, the indicators of progress it will monitor, and the specific ways each member of the organization can contribute both to its long-term purpose and short-term goals. (p. 41)

Obviously, leadership is important, but leadership without focus can result in people working hard with no apparent purpose or direction. At White River, we knew what we called "leadership by doing" had to be our method for improvement. We realized that if we expected school grade-level and content teams to implement best practices and make data-driven decisions, we would need to model that work at the district level in our district leadership team meetings. Monthly district leadership team meetings became the vehicle to make this happen. The organization and work of the district leadership team is based on the following assumptions.

In White River, the district leadership team models the work members expect of the building leadership team in the building. As we showed in the introduction (figure I.1, page 10), this work includes the following actions.

- Collaboratively develop role definitions and shared commitments.

- Create team norms and accountability protocols.

- Focus on learning.

- Establish regular meetings and agendas.

- Practice and rehearse the work.

- Anticipate questions and issues.

- Examine the work of high-performing teacher teams.

- Engage in shared learning.

- Share learning data.

- Set individual building commitments based on the work from learning meetings.

- Determine evidence for the next meeting that demonstrates progress toward meeting the commitments.

- Monitor results and expect continuous improvement.

- Model the behaviors expected of others.

- Celebrate improvement.

These important actions are not possible if principals are not viewed as district leaders within a PLC.

Principals Must Be District Leaders

In many districts, principals do not view themselves as part of district leadership, and they also do not view themselves as part of their school's staff. They often view themselves much like a matador passing a bull through his cape. They see their role as passing along information from the district office. After a traditional district office principals' meeting, it is not uncommon to hear a principal announce at the next faculty meeting, "They (the superintendent and district office) want you to . . . . Now, I'm just relaying to you what they said. It's coming from them, not me. I'm just the messenger here." Such a view is problematic as it divorces principals from taking responsibility for success regarding any decision or initiative that originates from the district office.

In the White River School District, we believe that pronouns matter; when principals refer to the district office, we prefer they use the pronoun *we* to the pronoun *they*. To embed a culture of shared ownership and shared responsibility throughout the district, principals are part of the district leadership team. When a principal returns to his or her individual school to communicate with the faculty about a decision that has been made at a district meeting, he or she accepts ownership of district decisions and initiatives because he or she is an integral member of the district leadership team.

Principals Must Communicate an Accurate and Compelling Why and How

If we are truly committed to improving learning for all students in our schools, we must embrace and articulate the expectation that every student is capable of learning at high levels. We define that as meeting grade-level standards and above, and it represents the why of the work in a PLC.

The Why

In the White River School District, we also needed to take a stand about how we were talking about students, and the principal is at the forefront of this process. He or she has to call out comments such as, "That child is low!"; "That's a red student!"; "Those are the bubble kids."; or, "That's a sped-er!" and lead the school in recognizing that the words we use about students frame how we think about them. Principals must internalize that their work and conversations about students need to reflect the question, "Is this good enough for my child?" (Eaker & Keating, 2015, p. 42).

Staff members would want any discussion about their child to first and foremost focus on the child's strengths. They would then want the conversation to highlight the learning that Tier 1, Tier 2, and Tier 3 will address during instruction and intervention—not on the perceived weaknesses of individual students.

We also realized that it was important for principals to tackle staff members' flawed student-learning assumptions. For example, when staff members make statements such as, "The students at X school are smarter than the students at my school," the necessary response is to ask staff, "Are the students smarter, or are they better prepared?" If students in the other geographic area are inherently smarter, then every parent in the district should move to get the same results. Parents, sell your house and move across town! That's obviously not the answer to having students meet grade-level standards.

What district leadership teams must do instead is create a compelling why that includes presenting school-level teams with accurate data. The school-by-school data in White River showed that our kindergarten students arrived for the first day of school in pretty much the same place academically, but they looked distinctly different by the end of the kindergarten year. The discrepancies were even larger by the end of second grade. The data provided a lens that helped teams understand that a student's address isn't the issue; rather, what makes the difference in student achievement is what the principal and collaborative teacher teams do daily—the collective efficacy of the school teams:

> When educators share a sense of collective efficacy, school cultures tend to be characterized by beliefs that reflect high expectations for student success. A shared language that represents a focus on student learning as opposed to instructional compliance often emerges. The perceptions that influence the actions of educators include "We are evaluators," "We are change agents," and "We collaborate." Teachers and leaders believe that it is their fundamental task to evaluate the effect of their practice on students' progress and achievement. (Donohoo, Hattie, & Eells, 2018, p. 41)

In White River, we needed to acknowledge that in some of our schools, we had what we called a *pipeline issue*. This term refers to the connection between grade levels in a school or the entire district. If the teachers at a lower grade level do not adequately prepare their students for the next grade level by ensuring that the students master essential standards, the higher grade-level teachers will need to provide Tier 3 intervention on the previous grade-level standards as well as teach their current grade-level standards.

We needed to recognize this fact and own it—no excuses. Pipeline issues aren't always an easy thing for educators to accept. For example, some school-level collaborative teams in White River shared openly that they believed the district office was blaming the kindergarten to grade 2 teachers for poor state assessment scores; however, the district leadership team communicated a difficult truth: "We understand how you could interpret our comments as blaming you; but what we are doing is pointing out the facts—highlighting the data. We didn't manufacture the data!"

One White River elementary principal asked for more detailed data to share with his building leadership team to express to teacher teams White River's pipeline issue. In response, the district leadership team created a straightforward spreadsheet for each grade that contained *student-by-student* benchmark data, color coded to highlight students who were below the 40th percentile. It included benchmark data for each year of a student's schooling; so, for example, the third-grade students had kindergarten, first-, and second-grade data as well as their fall third-grade benchmark. The data made it very clear to everyone that if a student leaves kindergarten with a spring benchmark score below the 40th percentile in national ranking, the student will continue to struggle academically in first grade, second grade, third grade, and so on. In other words, if a student develops a gap in kindergarten, or we couldn't close a gap for a student who wasn't kindergarten ready, the odds are that that gap will continue to widen through elementary and into middle and high school. We doubt this pattern is unique to White River.

It is morally unacceptable to allow students to believe they are not capable when in fact it is often educators who have not done their job. For us, the data were incontrovertible. Our kindergarten through grade 2 teachers needed to focus on results. They needed to be clear about the essential standards and target Tier 2 and Tier 3 intervention and remediation accordingly.

The first-grade team at the White River school where the principal requested the data from the district leadership team took this to heart, and this fact showed in the team's benchmark results that spring. They focused intently on whether each student was achieving the essential standards. They ensured that they tied Tier 2 interventions to core instruction and that students who needed Tier 3 remediation for skill gaps that they entered first grade with received that intervention.

The previous year the team had 29 percent—nearly one-third of their students—still needing Tier 3 remediation in the spring, with another 10 percent requiring Tier 2 intervention. Their intentional work brought those numbers down to 17 percent requiring Tier 3 remediation and only 6 percent requiring Tier 2 intervention. There is more work to be done, but the team—with the help and support of the district leadership team—is on the right path.

The point is, every school district needs to address misconceptions related to student learning. It is the responsibility of all the adults and every team in the school to provide the necessary conditions so learning *for all* can occur. The district leadership team reviews student learning data throughout the year, just as the teacher collaborative teams do on a weekly basis. This team needs to be deeply curious about learning data and ask questions when learning discrepancies occur from grade to grade or building to building. This shared learning will allow the district leadership team to identify best practices in areas where learning goals are being met and to set expectations for future growth. This process models the conversations that principals will be expected to have with their building leadership team when they review learning data at their school.

Authors Anthony Muhammad and Sharroky Hollie (2012) state that to bring a mission statement to life, "educators must be willing to transparently communicate their commitment to students as it relates to their stated mission and challenge one another to live up to that commitment" (p. 28). A school's mission communicates in what direction each staff member needs to be heading. After the why, the next point of discussion from principals with the support of the district leadership team needs to be about how to measure success. Establishing the why is the result of collaborative analysis of data. Data-based decision making helps align actions with the district's mission.

The How

After focusing on the why, the district leadership team must focus on the how. What this means is that teacher teams, with the support of the district leadership team, need to identify how they will know they have achieved success and monitor whether what they are doing is getting them there. As DuFour and colleagues (2016) point out, principals address this issue by asking the faculty to "identify the indicators that should be monitored to assess the progress they made in creating their agreed-upon school" and establish benchmarks "for what they hoped to achieve in the first six months, the first year, and the first three years" (p. 23).

The district office via the district leadership team works with principals to monitor the data at critical points during the year so it can respond directly to student learning needs. For example, the team meets with each principal individually to review benchmark data in early September—kid by kid and skill by skill. The reading and mathematics benchmark data are valuable because they represent a nationally normed assessment—an external measure to check in and catch students who are missing universal skills and may struggle to interact with grade-level standards. This is a time when the team looks at each school's master schedule again to make sure it provides appropriate time for Tier 2 and Tier 3 supports without taking students out of essential Tier 1 instruction. (It isn't possible to close the gap for students if they are never learning grade-level standards. We can't expect a third grader to meet state standards if he or she has never even seen those standards.)

In January, the team comes back together with the principals to examine growth between fall and winter benchmark data, alongside English language arts units 1 and 2, and mathematics units 1, 2, and 3. At the middle and high school level, the team is looking at data from key coursework, including the universal skills and the grade-level standards. This might be a time when the district office makes some decisions to deploy extra support to a building based on the data. For example, the district leadership team at White River has added paraeducator support for specific buildings based on data during this January meeting. The team has also created additional time with this data check-in for principals to do the work of a professional learning community—learning from each other. If one or several schools are making significant progress, the other principals need to learn about the practices in those schools immediately. The data and purposeful conversations surrounding them give leaders time to share strategies and work with their school-level teams prior to the beginning of the second semester.

At White River, the final district leadership team meeting of the year happens in June. At this point in the year, the team has examined three benchmark points, unit assessment data, 90 percent reading goal data for first and second grade, and state assessment results. If the summative assessment data are not what the team expected, principals and their collaborative teacher teams need to reflect on why this came as a surprise. Do unit assessments actually align and predict student achievement as measured by state assessments? Is your data tracking system effective (are you misidentifying students who have achievement gaps)?

This end-of-year meeting is also when the team begins planning for the following school year. Why wait until six weeks into the start of next school year to begin interventions when we already know which students will need support? All this work between the district and building principals keeps the compelling why in the forefront daily while addressing the how. It keeps the focus on the why and how instead of allowing management-related tasks to take over.

Connecting the Why and How

Consider the following example of connecting the why to the work of improving student learning from an assistant superintendent—Greg Upham—in the Helena School District in Montana. He and his district leadership team created what they call the *Why Tour*. The team visited every school and presented big-picture district data and school-by-school data surrounding student learning and achievement. This examination revealed the facts about the high numbers of students performing below expectations and the significant number of students not graduating from high school. Greg stated to each school and staff member, "We are better than this! Our kids deserve better than this" (G. Upham, personal communication, July 22, 2019).

Accurate student learning data set the stage for the answer to the question, Why change? Let the data be a powerful force to create a compelling why for change in practice. Greg and his team knew that they had to pay close attention to the fundamentals: core instruction in the classroom, and Tier 2 and Tier 3 interventions tied to universal skills.

The team also had to have the political will to stand firm when the system fights to maintain complacency. Greg presented the why for urgency in the work, and then provided the how—the time and support for teams to do the work. Kelley Edwards, a teacher in the Helena School District, put it this way:

> Research shows that teachers working together can have a profound impact on student learning, and my experience was no exception. Professional Learning Communities (PLC) allowed me to become a more reflective teacher by utilizing data and best practice methods to improve student achievement. The PLC process allowed us, for the first time, to make the fundamental shift from "my students" to "our students." Setting a collective goal, sharing our frustrations and success, and striving always to improve, ultimately led to higher student achievement. (K. Edwards, personal communication, July 22, 2019)

The Helena School District has made impressive improvements by implementing the concepts and practices of the PLC process. Their work is highlighted in *Clarity: What Matters Most in Learning, Teaching, and Leading* (Sharratt, 2019). Helena modeled much of its work after the work in White River. Greg Upham continues to lead this great work as superintendent in Billings, Montana, the largest school system in the state of Montana.

Principals Must Know the Work Deeply

Since the 1970s, the research on effective schools has highlighted the critical role of principals. According to the Wallace Foundation Report (2009), "Effective leadership is vital to the success of a school. Research and practice confirm that there is a slim chance of creating and sustaining high-quality learning environments without a skilled and committed leader to help shape teaching and learning" (p. 1).

Several studies back up the Wallace Foundation's claim, noting school leadership as second to classroom instruction as a primary driver for student performance, both positive and negative. In particular, the body of research indicates principals have the greatest impact on student achievement in schools with the greatest needs (for example, high poverty rates, low student attendance, low graduation rates, and high teacher turnover). Furthermore, principal leadership is the most important factor for attracting and retaining quality teachers. Research indicates that the main reason teachers choose whether or not to stay in a particular school is the quality of support they receive from their principal. Overall, schools require principals who are capable of collaboratively crafting a vision for student success, cultivating a student-centered culture, building others' leadership capacity, improving instruction, and leading school improvement efforts. Essentially, effective principals lead effective schools.

In the White River School District, principals are considered the primary change agent in every school, with the responsibility to stretch the aspirations and performance of every team in their building. DuFour (2015) echoes the important role of the building principal when he writes:

> It is certainly easier for principals to merely manage the building, preserve the status quo, and avoid creating discomfort. For too long,

too many principals have chosen the easier path. But if we are to create schools committed to helping all students learn at higher levels, American schools need principals who have the courage to move beyond managing to leading and developing the leadership capacity of many others, principals who can build consensus for substantive change and work through the inevitable discomfort, and principals who accept there will be times when they must settle for less than universal affection from their staff. Those who take this path less chosen will embrace and articulate the moral imperative of ensuring high levels of learning for all students and will acknowledge that creating the conditions for addressing that imperative lies within their sphere of influence. (p. 247)

DuFour (2015), in *In Praise of American Educators*, shares a specific list of responsibilities to guide the work of principals:

- Clarify the purpose, vision, collective commitments, and goals that define your school.

- Create a culture that is simultaneously loose and tight, and clearly communicate the purpose and priorities of your school.

- Use the collaborative team as the fundamental structure of your school, and put systems in place to facilitate and support the collaborative team process.

- Ensure that students have access to a guaranteed and viable curriculum unit by unit.

- Monitor each student's learning through an ongoing assessment process that includes multiple team-developed common formative assessments.

- Provide every teacher and team with access to ongoing evidence of student learning, and ensure they use that evidence to inform and improve their individual and collective practices.

- Provide students who struggle with additional time and support for learning in a way that is timely, directive, precise, and systematic, and provide students who are proficient with opportunities for extension and enrichment.

- Demonstrate reciprocal accountability by providing staff members with the time, resources, and support that enable them to succeed at what you are asking them to do.

- Disperse leadership throughout the school, and build such a strong collaborative culture that those other leaders can continue the PLC journey long after you have left the school.

- Persevere in the face of obstacles and setbacks, and never lose faith that your efforts and the collective efforts of the staff can overcome those challenges and ultimately lead to higher levels of student achievement.

- Stay the course. (pp. 245–247)

We would also add the following three actions.

1. Ensure that there is a systemic approach to Tier 1 instruction for all students that proactively addresses barriers and Tier 2, and Tier 3 interventions tied to essential standards through the RTI/MTSS process.

2. Establish and monitor student growth goals aligned to the essential standards.

3. Create a multi-tiered system of support that facilitates the process of collecting and monitoring academic, behavioral, and social-emotional data collected, unit by unit, to ensure that individual student needs are addressed in a timely manner.

These three actions represent what we defined earlier in this book as glass balls for principal leadership—the leadership behaviors and actions that can't be dropped or delegated—as opposed to the rubber balls in the principal role, which are management tasks. If a glass ball drops, it shatters; when a leader drops a glass ball it results in negative effects on student learning. A master schedule that provides time for Tier 1 core instruction for all students (with no pull-outs), as well as Tier 2 and Tier 3 intervention, is an example of a glass ball. If a principal doesn't have a master schedule in place that meets these requirements, it will negatively impact the learning of every student in the school.

Let's revisit the quote from DuFour (2015): "The job of principal is daunting yet doable" (p. 247).

How can the district office make the job of the principal doable, and ensure that it has a positive impact on student learning? In White River School District, the district leadership team focused its efforts on developing a way to think about operationalizing the glass balls. For example, we felt it was essential for principals to spend time learning the scope and sequence of essential standards for each grade level and content area they supervise. Elementary principals need to know when important concepts like fractions are being taught in fourth grade. Finding equivalent fractions and comparing fractions are both essential skills, especially moving into fifth grade. Elementary school principals need to know what percentage of the state assessment is made up of fraction concepts. They can become knowledgeable about this by reviewing the assessment blueprint, the test item specifications, and the test question stems. Even career and technical education courses have an assessment blueprint connected to the industry-recognized CTE certifications.

Principals also need to spend time with school grade-level and content teams, discussing what these grade-level standards mean and what they look like in student work. They need to engage with school grade-level and content teams about lesson design and effective instructional strategies tied to these standards. Teacher observations and feedback need to be aligned with what's most important. That means principals need to intentionally put this critical information on their calendars. Often, we hear principals say to teachers, "I need to observe you in the next two weeks. What do you want me to see?" This is an example of a "compliance with the contract" conversation, not a conversation geared toward improving student learning. Remember, effective leaders pay attention to and give feedback on what is essential. They lead with the essential standard first and all their work is aligned to student achievement of the essential standards. These principals communicate schoolwide about what standards are being taught, learned, and assessed. You can find them in the hallway and staff room engaged in conversation with the teacher or teacher team about student learning based on the essential standard. The end of unit assessment date is on their calendar—it's an important event. The first question will be, Did the team members meet their unit SMART goal?

During Monday late-start collaboration time within individual schools in White River, principals should not be sitting in their offices; they should be at the table with teams, listening to discussions about the guaranteed and viable curriculum, observing as teams analyze the data on student work, and seeing the plans for Tier 2 intervention as well as extension. Principals won't be able to attend every collaborative team meeting. When returning to their offices after collaboration, they can review each team's monthly planning tool. (We share this tool, collaboratively developed by the district leadership team, in chapter 4, page 91.) Here teams highlight what they accomplished during collaboration time. They often link to a product such as a unit plan or the results of a common formative assessment. At White River, this planning tool is housed in our Google Drive, and principals can use the comment feature to give teams feedback on their products and progress. This tool provides two-way communication, as teams can also add a request for specific support from the principal. At every district leadership team meeting, the principals analyze data or examine a specific product of a teacher collaborative team. For example, analyzing the results of a fifth-grade end-of-unit mathematics common formative assessment is an agenda item. The principals can go to the Google Drive, open up the monthly planning tool and the unit plan, and then the TACA. They won't have to prepare for this meeting. The information each principal needs to bring or access for the meeting is right there. During the meeting, the principals will analyze the results of each fifth-grade team from each school. Together, they will learn where the fifth-grade students across the district did well, what strategies helped the students do well, and where students are struggling. This principal team is now looking and acting like a collaborative team in a PLC. The middle school principal is at the table with the elementary principals since these fifth-grade students will be at the middle school next year. The middle school principal is interested in the results and invested in their success.

Paying attention to the products school-level teams generate is a critical step to improve learning in a school. In some districts, leaders require teams to turn in notes from collaborative meetings. Writing and reading meeting minutes, however, will never improve learning in a school. If you are a principal in a school with an assistant principal, it is valuable to establish a weekly time to meet for the purpose of discussing what each leader observed during collaborative time. This provides an opportunity to share examples of team products, highlight student-learning data, and brainstorm ways to help any teams that are struggling. Each leader has responsibility for monitoring the work of teams.

When a principal clearly understands the scope and sequence of instruction, or is clear on what happened during collaboration meetings, classroom visits are more informative and purposeful. Principals should be visiting classrooms daily to check in with students and to observe, monitor, and support the work surrounding the guaranteed and viable curriculum—the work discussed during collaboration. Does the work of collaborative teacher teams come alive in the classroom? For example, are the interventions collaborative teams have discussed observable in the classroom? Consider this note that Cody Mothershead, the principal of White River High School, sent to his algebra team:

> Today, the algebra team worked together to use formative assessment data from last week to identify students who are still struggling with the same skill. Catherine held a closed Hornet time intervention today with a combination of students from her class, Strydar's, Brandon's, and Brad's classes. Catherine had a packed room with about thirty-four students in which she taught a mini lesson on a specific skill of graphing quadratic equations. There were no behavior issues and students were engaged and working. I heard comments like "I get this now; it helps hearing it in a different way from a different teacher" and, "Can I come back again for help like this?" This is a great example of the team working together to support all kids and not just "my kids." Thank you, Algebra team, for your collaborative work to support students. This is exactly the work we should be doing every Monday and a fantastic example of working together on behalf of our kids. This process works and helps support all students. (C. Mothershead, personal communication, February 5, 2020)

This note shows that the principal understands the work teachers are doing deeply and can connect it to the why of the work. Importantly, when principals know the work deeply and communicate progress to the district leadership team, they are better able to plan, monitor, and support professional development for school-level collaborative teams.

Principals Must Plan, Monitor, and Support Professional Development

At White River, we believe that developing the leadership capacity of all principals in the district is an important part of the job of those in the district office. This means that district leaders have strong reciprocal accountability for principal learning and success. At White River, we don't simply assume that new or veteran principals have the capacity to create conditions for addressing the moral imperative of ensuring high levels of learning for all students. We create systems that support their growth so that they are set up to successfully support their staff's growth.

Just as we know that each student in a classroom can be at a different place in his or her learning, and that each team in a school may need different types of support, so we also know that our principals and school leaders may need different levels of support. Even principals need extra time, support, and extension of their learning.

In White River, we use district leadership team meetings as a place to learn together. The framework for this learning is always the four critical questions of a PLC: (1) what do we want students to know and be able to do? (2) how do we know when they have learned it? (3) how will we respond when some students have not learned it? and (4) how will we extend the learning for students who have demonstrated proficiency? (DuFour et al., 2016). District leaders should not expect that principals, or anyone else, just *knows* best practice in all aspects of the work; they can, however, rightfully expect that principals are willing and able to learn. The questions provide the filter the district leadership team uses to improve learning, prevent initiative overload, and stay focused on the right work.

The following is an example of how White River teams layer the work for each critical question.

1. **What do we want students to know and be able to do?** Teams examine Common Core State Standards (CCSS), CTE industry standards, social-emotional learning, essential standards, power standards, priority standards, learning targets, pacing, clarifying standards (what standards look like in student work), proficiency scales, lesson design, instructional strategies and engagement, rigor, and social-emotional learning.

   At White River, the district leadership team engaged in a book study of *Focus: Elevating the Essentials to Radically Improve Student Learning,* second edition, by Mike Schmoker (2009). Each building team read chapter 2, "What We Teach" and chapter 3, "How We Teach." The purpose of the book study was to review the components of a guaranteed and viable curriculum and for each building leadership team to identify the components of effective lessons. Each building leadership team was then tasked to identify next steps for supporting the teacher teams in their building. Building leadership teams then created a written plan that was shared with the larger district leadership team and implemented in their building over the next month. At the next scheduled meeting, each building leadership team shared progress and evidence of improvement.

2. **How do we know when they have learned it?** Teams look at benchmark assessments, preassessments, common formative end-of-unit assessments, in-unit quick checks for understanding, state assessments, SAT, ACT, and results analysis.

3. **How will we respond when some students have not learned it?** Teams implement differentiated instruction, Tier 2 close-to-core interventions, Tier 3 remediation, PBIS, MTSS, and AVID.

4. **How will we extend the learning for students who have demonstrated proficiency?** Teams implement differentiated instruction and increased rigor involving higher-order thinking.

Professional development for the district leadership team is based on needs that surface from common formative assessment data, the state assessment data, or an element of the work that addresses the four PLC critical questions. This team tackles the learning first. For example, if the data tell us that our students need to do more writing grounded in evidence from informational text, professional development during the district leadership team meeting will address this area. The team will study, practice, and rehearse the work together. Prior to each team member leaving the meeting, he or she will commit to next steps with his or her building leadership team based on the leaning from that specific meeting. They also commit to what evidence from their next step they will bring to the next district leadership team meeting.

Include Teacher Leaders: The Building Learning Coordinator

When we began to implement the concepts and practices of the PLC process throughout White River School District, it became apparent that our implementation was uneven. Even with steady training during district leadership team meetings, we weren't achieving consistent implementation across the district.

We discovered that although we had created an administrator and principal learning community during the district leadership team monthly meetings, when principals returned to their buildings they were back to leading in isolation. We mistakenly assumed they all understood the work and were prepared to share and teach it to their staff.

The graphic in figure 2.1 is a model of how school leadership has traditionally been arranged and how information traditionally flows.

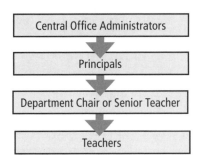

Figure 2.1: Traditional model of information flow within a school district.

At White River, we re-examined our district leadership structure and realized we had a missing link: the connection between the principal and the building staff. To create this link, we established the building learning coordinator position. The building learning coordinator is a full-time teacher who receives a stipend to work side by side with the principal, building leadership team, and the teacher collaborative grade-level or content teams. The building learning coordinator helps coordinate the work that happens in the district leadership team meetings with that of the building leadership team meetings and with that of the teacher collaborative teams. The goal is to never have a teacher team say, "Why are we doing this?" or "How do they want us to analyze our data?"

The graphic in figure 2.2 shows how our system works in White River School District. Information flows in both directions, and at every level, teams include teachers as well as administrators.

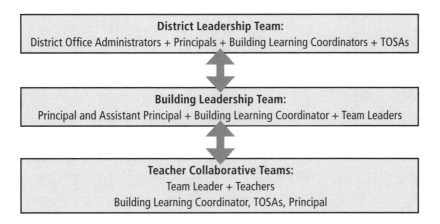

Figure 2.2: Flow of information in White River School District.

The building learning coordinator receives a half-day substitute teacher monthly to attend the district leadership team meeting. The primary function of this position is to enhance teacher and team capacity to improve student learning. All of these teachers must have a demonstrated record of exceptional teaching skills as reflected in the high learning levels of their students, as well as the earned respect of their peers. These are teachers who have influence with the building staff. They will ensure that teams focus on the four critical questions of learning and enhance the effectiveness of each team. The building learning coordinator's professional behavior must support all aspects of the district vision and direction. By the time the work lands on the table of the teacher team, it has intentionally been practiced and rehearsed at the district leadership team meeting, as well as the building leadership team meeting.

The building learning coordinator position is of critical importance as the White River School District continues to sharpen its focus on improving student learning levels through PLC practices. The educators who fill these positions work side by side with the principal and closely with school grade-level and content teams by coordinating with the team leader at each grade level or content area. Building learning coordinators work with school grade-level and content teams to review student learning data, analyze student work, lead teams in reflective practice, share with individual teachers and teams proven best practices for enhancing student learning, and assist teams in setting and achieving learning-based SMART goals. They ensure that teams focus on the critical questions of learning in a high-quality way.

Additionally, building learning coordinators focus on improving the effectiveness of each team. Recognizing that teams, like students, learn at different rates and in different ways, they model *differentiated teaming*; teams may struggle for different reasons and have different needs. The building learning coordinator provides detailed support when teams struggle. For example, a team may not understand why it is important to bring student achievement data to the weekly team meeting. The building learning coordinator can guide the team through a process to understand which students have not mastered the essential learning targets for the purpose of planning, reteaching, and interventions.

Building learning coordinators must understand how effective teams function and how to enhance team capacity. In short, working side by side with their principals, they are responsible for helping each team function more efficiently and more effectively. Recognizing that professional development in a school that functions as a high-performing PLC differs significantly from more traditional schools, the building learning coordinator works with each team to assess professional development needs and assist the principal and team leaders in developing and monitoring the professional development plan that is embedded in the school improvement plan.

Excellent technology and interpersonal skills are critical for this position. Building learning coordinators must work well with others, possessing the skills to work with a variety of groups and individuals, while at the same time demonstrating results.

An important caveat is in order here: simply adding a building learning coordinator will not, in and of itself, improve learning. To make a difference, there must be clear expectations regarding how this position operates at the district and school level. First, building learning coordinators must attend and participate in all district leadership team meetings. They must also attend the administrative summer retreat. In White River, we rarely have a meeting in the district without these teacher leaders present. We believe they help us make better decisions about student learning. Building learning coordinators attend the monthly district leadership meetings as well as the building leadership team meetings in their building. If there is a meeting focused on student learning, the building learning coordinators are at the table.

Also, principals need to be able to place their trust in these teacher leaders. Principals rely on the building learning coordinator to bring the teaching lens—the teacher perspective—to the work that happens at the district leadership team meetings, building leadership team meetings, and finally to the school grade-level and content team meetings.

These teacher leaders help administrators practice and rehearse the work that teams are expected to do. At times, they teach administrators *how* to do the work. After all, they're in the classroom daily working with students. You could say these teacher leaders make administrators smarter, and they do. For this position to have any leverage on adult and student learning, there must be agreed-on expectations, processes, and practices regarding the relationship between the principal and building learning coordinator.

Consider the work of Chris Schumacher, White River High School's building learning coordinator. Every week, Chris joins the principal to work with teams around best practices, such as implementing interactive notebooks, lesson design, and data collection to facilitate instruction and intervention. She then works with individual teams to take a deep dive into specific practices. For example, the school focus for lesson design was on creating entry and exit tasks to begin and end lessons. One of the positive things about this focus was its value for all areas of study, whether you're working with a mathematics team or a singleton culinary teacher. Both need ways to check for student understanding through entry and exit tasks, and they can use the information to drive both instruction and interventions for the next day or week. It's a district expectation that the principal and building learning coordinator collaborate to impact the work of every team and singleton teacher in the school.

Meeting once a week is an expectation and an agreed-on practice between all principals and building learning coordinators. Principals count on the building learning coordinator to bring the teacher point of view since they are in the classroom improving learning kid by kid and skill by skill.

Drill Deeper With Focused Teamwork

Our monthly district leadership team meetings became the vehicles to make our mission, vision, values (collective commitments), and goals come alive on a districtwide basis. We created a system where, each month, district leaders drilled deeper into the knowledge base and understanding of the concepts and practices of the PLC process in order to effectively lead the work of improving learning districtwide—school by school, team by team, student by student, and skill by skill. Together we learned how to identify essential standards, deconstruct a standard into learning targets, and create common formative assessments. We also tackled difficult district conversations about effective grading and reporting practices. The district leadership team also learned to craft and monitor the progress of each team's SMART goals.

Importantly, we practiced and rehearsed the work principals would be leading in their schools. Together, we anticipated issues that might arise and the questions that school grade-level and content teams might have regarding the work. We sought to create an environment within the team where principals learned and asked clarifying questions. For example, if our goal was to ensure that school grade-level and content teams understand the connection between the learning target, the common formative assessments, and additional time, support, and extension, we shared examples and worked on making those connections. We worked together through multiple examples at each level—elementary, middle, and high school. Consider the high school example in figure 2.3 (page 66) that shows how our high school algebra team broke down learning targets.

Again, district leadership team meetings provide time for principals to ask questions and anticipate any issues they might have while doing the work with teams at their schools. This practicing and rehearsing of the work that school grade-level and content teams will eventually do allows principals to work the kinks out before taking the work back to their school-level teams. It is also a valuable opportunity to learn from each other.

Observing the work of an effective team remains a consistent agenda item on the district leadership team. The superintendent (or a designee) selects an effective team based on the work principals have observed during weekly collaboration time or based on a product in the shared worksite. This team is selected to showcase a piece of its work. Essentially, members of the district leadership team use the fishbowl process to observe a grade-level or content team replicating its collaborative work.

Sequential Learning Targets	
I can write and solve one-step equations for a single variable by adding or subtracting (using algebra tiles).	*1 day*
This means I can . . . ✓ Apply the additive identity property ✓ Model an equation symbolically or with algebra tiles (ensure we use to create visual for students) ✓ Write an equation to represent a given scenario	
One-Step Equations (Kuta worksheet; www.kutasoftware.com)	
Entry task: Give exit slip as entrance task to see how students do, and then ask them to make any changes needed as an exit slip.	
Exit task: Interim Assessment Block Exit Slip 1	
I can write and solve one-step equations for a single variable by multiplying or dividing (using algebra tiles).	*1 day*
This means I can . . . ✓ Apply the multiplicative identity property ✓ Model an equation symbolically or with algebra tiles (ensure we use to create visual for students) ✓ Write an equation to represent a given scenario	
Climb the Ladder—Solving Equations, Grade 6	
Formative *quiz on targets one and two;* add word problems on quiz.	

Source: White River School District, 2020. Used with permission.

Figure 2.3: Example showing how an algebra team broke down learning targets.

The district office staff, principals, and building learning coordinators from every building are seated on the perimeter of the team they will observe. This team is seated at a table in the center of the room. We might observe a team deconstructing a standard into learning targets. It could be a team creating the end-of-unit common formative assessment or a team analyzing the results of a formative assessment and forming intervention or extension groups.

During this activity, administrators are observing best practice and can then engage in the benchmarking activity. Through benchmarking, principals reflect on the work they just observed and ask, "Does the work I just observed reflect the kind of work and quality of work of the school grade-level and content teams at my school?" This fishbowl process also provides an opportunity to give feedback to the observed grade-level or content team. Even a high-performing team has room for improvement.

At the close of every district leadership team meeting, members ask the same questions: "Based on what you learned today, what are you committed to working on or doing with your building leadership team and your school grade-level and content teams? At next month's meeting, what product or products are you committed to bring back as evidence of doing the work?"

These commitments could be as simple as an exit slip or a quick email to the superintendent or assistant superintendent. For the next month, every conversation district office leaders have with individual principals is focused on supporting their commitments. When district office leaders visit school buildings, they don't ask, "How's it going?" They ask questions and review products and student learning data specifically related to the principals' commitments.

District leaders monitor the data with principals, unit by unit. The district office support is directly aligned, helping each principal accomplish the work related to his or her commitments. White River has found value in this strategy of positive peer pressure.

In the White River School District, we believe in learning from each other and in making our work transparent—the same expectations school leaders have for members of school grade-level and content teams. For example, if you were to attend a district leadership team meeting, you might be quickly engaged in a gallery walk, viewing examples of the commitments from the month before, or you might observe a team of elementary or secondary principals sharing products related to the previous month's commitments. Leaders should ask each other probing questions with the goal of continuous improvement. All schools' administrative teams and building learning coordinators should show up to each meeting with evidence of what their building leadership team and school grade-level and content teams accomplished related to the previous month's commitment. Principals then have time to discuss the products and evidence and give feedback.

The practices of the district level and principal team within its meetings give leaders the opportunity to look and act like a PLC. It is not uncommon for leaders to examine the critical elements of a unit plan, review a common assessment, or discuss the results of an end-of-unit common formative assessment.

You might be thinking to yourself, How does the team handle the nuts and bolts? When nuts-and-bolts items are placed first on the agenda, they take longer than anticipated and the team runs out of time to tackle the most important part of the meeting—improving learning and leadership. At White River, we don't allow the nuts-and-bolts items to trump items on the agenda that will improve learning. They are either placed at the end of the agenda where time constraints force them to be dealt with quickly, or handled in email or elsewhere.

Meetings are costly. If a district leadership team meeting is scheduled to take three or four hours, that is a very high cost. Do the math; add up the salaries of all the people in the room—some of the highest-paid district employees. Given this, it's no surprise that everything on the agenda should involve an impact on learning across the district.

Focus on Principal Leadership

The relationship between effective school leadership and increased student achievement is documented. Research by the Wallace Foundation (2013) indicates:

> A particularly noteworthy finding . . . is the empirical link between school leadership and improved student achievement. . . . The research shows that most school variables, considered separately, have at most small effects on learning. The real payoff comes when individual variables combine to reach critical mass. Creating the conditions under

which that can occur is the job of the principal. Indeed, leadership is second only to classroom instruction among school-related factors that affect student learning in school. (p. 5)

In White River, we recognize most school improvement efforts in Washington State and across the United States focus first on teachers to include teacher evaluation, or a new instructional framework. We believe a school is probably not going to be any better than its principal. If the principal doesn't understand the work or hasn't personally experienced the work, the school is in trouble. Think about it like this: if what students in the classroom learn is due in part to the quality of the teacher, then it only makes sense that the quality of the work of the school grade-level and content teams would depend to a great extent on the knowledge base of the principal. The principal must know the right work and embed the work in every team, and the quality of the principal's work is to some extent determined by the quality of support from the district office. As Douglas Reeves and Robert Eaker (2019) point out, "In many schools, teacher teams are typically asked to successfully complete tasks that principals have never experienced themselves" (p. 90). But in schools striving to align PLC practices districtwide, principals must first ensure that "they understand and can do the work themselves before tasking teacher teams. This increases the principal's credibility with staff, of course, but more importantly, it improves the principal's ability to assist struggling teams." (Reeves & Eaker, 2019, p. 90)

In White River School District, we made a conscious effort to improve the quality of principal leadership. We want our principals to be equipped to help their teachers and to *learn with them* versus simply *direct them*. There are many school principals who direct work that they don't know how to do themselves. They actually slow the teachers' work down. In the past, principals would make comments like, "I can't have my staff do that work yet. I'm working on culture." The best way to work on culture is to give your teachers a new, successful experience. Organize your school into collaborative teams, require teams to do the work of a PLC, and celebrate their success. The intentional work of a team and the belief that student learning is within our locus of control will change the culture.

Consider this quote by Muhammad and Cruz (2019):

> A healthy school culture produces a professional environment in which educators unwaveringly believe that all students can achieve academic and social success, and they overtly and covertly communicate that expectation to others. Educators in these environments are willing to create policies, practices, and procedures that align with their beliefs and are rooted in their confidence in universal student achievement. To paraphrase, educators in a healthy school culture believe that all students can excel, and they willingly challenge and change their own practices to meet that end. (p. 14)

Muhammad and Cruz (2019) go on to share:

> A healthy culture operates from two important assumptions. The first expects that everyone within the organization believes that students can and will learn at high levels. The second assumption is that the

educators who work within a healthy culture are willing to change or adjust their behavior based on objective evidence about student growth and development. (p. 15)

Celebrate Successes Along the Journey

Frequent and timely celebrations are important for communicating what is truly valued in the White River School District. Our district leadership team meetings are designed to seek best practice and to model, practice, and celebrate the work we expect of the school grade-level and content teams in each school.

If you were to drop in on a district leadership team meeting, you would see some consistent themes. Every meeting starts with a celebration. For example, White River has a "Save the Shoes" award. This award recognizes a leader whose actions have made a significant impact on learning.

In his March 2011 Ted Talk, volunteer firefighter Mark Bezos tells the story of the second fire he responded to: by the time he arrived, the "real" firefighters had pretty much put out the fire. The chief sent a firefighter into the house to get the family dog and assigned Mark to find a pair of shoes for the homeowner, who was standing outside in the rain, barefoot in her nightclothes. In the moment, he felt crushed that he didn't have a more glamorous role to play. A few weeks later, the department received a letter from the homeowner, thanking them for the valiant effort displayed in saving her home. The act of kindness noted above all others: that a firefighter had even retrieved a pair of shoes for her.

Mark concludes by saying that in his life he is witness to acts of generosity and kindness on a monumental scale. But he also witnesses acts of grace and courage on an individual basis. He has learned that they all matter, so he offers this reminder:

> Don't wait until you make your first million to make a difference in somebody's life. If you have something to give, give it now. . . . Not every day is going to offer us a chance to save somebody's life, but every day offers us an opportunity to affect one. So, get in the game. Save the shoes. (Bezos, 2011)

Educators in White River are "saving shoes" every day, so we started a monthly Save the Shoes award a few years ago. The award goes to someone who has gone above and beyond the normal scope of his or her job to make a difference. One recipient, classroom teacher Nina Markey (now principal of Elk Ridge Elementary), exemplifies these heroics.

Nina ran the elementary Low Incidence Disability Program in the White River School District and also recently finished her administrative credentials. As part of her administrative internship, she helped the principal of her school organize a number of community events to keep people apprised of the bond projects in their building. Toward the end of the school year, she was also asked to step in and coteach with a fifth-grade teacher who was struggling. Nina took the task on without hesitation.

She made a difference for every student in that classroom and helped the teacher complete the school year feeling more successful. Nina truly exemplifies someone who sees a need and gives with a smile.

Another example of this Save the Shoes attitude in White River comes from the teacher recruiting efforts of Scott Harrison, director of human resources, and Mark Cushman, principal of Foothills Elementary. Most school districts attend teacher-recruiting events, meet and greet prospective candidates, and cross their fingers that the best ones will choose to apply in their districts. Scott and Mark exemplify our expectations of attracting the best teachers possible.

Scott spends countless hours communicating with student teaching supervisors at universities throughout the Pacific Northwest and the United States, encouraging them to have their candidates consider the White River School District. In some cases, he has multiple personal contacts with candidates who express interest in our district, or who have specific questions. He was relentless in setting up opportunities for building principals to attend teacher-recruiting fairs, and more importantly, making sure the principals' needs were met during those events. Scott leaves an unforgettable, positive impression on the candidates because of the standard of care and attention he provides to each one. He acts like he's hiring a teacher for his own children.

Mark Cushman is constantly recruiting teachers, not only for his building but also for the district. He will often tell a fellow principal that he has met or interviewed a candidate who would be a great fit in his or her building. He knows the district teams intimately and can find the best fit for a specific need. It is common practice for Mark to invite several candidates to Foothills Elementary to visit classrooms, talk with teachers, and have a conversation with him prior to the formal interview to help the candidate get a sense of what is important at White River and how we do our work. In addition, the questions candidates ask Mark and his staff provide insight into their observations and how they might see themselves fitting into the culture at Foothills Elementary or one of the other elementary schools in the district. Mark will easily spend four to eight hours with a candidate prior to an interview. He intentionally selects his interview questions to reflect collaborative attitudes and behaviors. For example, an interview prompt might be, "Tell me about a time when you've impacted the professional practice of a colleague or member of your team," or perhaps, "Tell me about a time when the professional practice of a colleague or team member impacted you."

In the White River School District, we believe that if we expect principals to celebrate learning and team accomplishments, then district leaders must celebrate in meaningful ways as well. As Rosabeth Moss Kanter (1999) writes:

> Remembering to recognize, reward, and celebrate accomplishments is a critical leadership skill. And it is probably the most underutilized motivational tool in organizations. There is no limit to how much recognition you can provide, and it is often free. Recognition brings the change cycle to its logical conclusion, but it also motivates people to change again. (p. 20)

The example in figure 2.4 shows the direct alignment between what happens at the district leadership team meetings and what happens at the building leadership team meetings (figure 2.5, page 72).

District Leadership Team Meeting

November 13

8:30–12:00

What do we want each student to learn?

How will we know if each student is learning it?

How will we respond when students experience difficulty?

How will we respond if the student already knows it?

8:30: Celebration—Save the Shoes Award

8:40: Leadership Commitments—Gallery Walk—View examples and products of your leadership commitments based on the work we did in our October meeting. Please provide written comments on two sample products.

9:00: Revisit SMART goals and the purpose of a SMART goal.

Part 1: Review SMART goal results from Unit 1 English language arts and mathematics at your level (elementary schools, Glacier Middle, and White River High School). Provide feedback to the teams on their goals.

Part 2: How is Aimsweb (benchmark screener) useful when setting SMART goals?

10:15: Break

10:30: Fishbowl of Mountain Meadow third-grade team using its unit plan to design weekly instruction

11:40: Establish leadership commitment

11:45: Nuts and bolts—spring conferences (Scott) and substitute coverage issues (elementary only)

Source: White River School District, 2020. Used with permission.

Figure 2.4: Sample district leadership team meeting agenda.

Conclusion

Richard DuFour and Robert Marzano (2011) emphasize the importance of principal leadership by stating, "Principals do indeed make a difference in student learning, and the most powerful strategy for having a positive impact on that learning is to facilitate the learning of the educators who serve these students through the PLC process" (p.63).

A high-performing district-level team that works closely with the principals and teacher leaders will create the structure for an effective system that moves student and adult learning forward across all schools. This is a piece of a successful PLC that is frequently overlooked. The next chapter is about how the principal operationalizes this work with his or her building leadership team, school by school.

White River High School Leadership Team Meeting Agenda
November 19

2:20 p.m. to 3:20 p.m.

Leadership Team Norms:

- We will not interrupt others; everyone should have the opportunity to share before someone speaks twice.

- Outcomes are transparent; the process is confidential.

- Be open and honest in conversations and assume good intentions.

- Decision making will be by consensus; when the will of the group is evident, we will move forward and support or assume ownership of the decision. The team will discuss how to share information.

Leadership Team Accountability Protocols:

- Review norms at each meeting.

- Evaluate norms twice per year to ensure they are effective for the group.

- Use the last five minutes of each meeting for self-reflection and accountability (self-report).

- Based on this meeting, what am I responsible for doing with my department or teams?

Clarity: Unit Plan and SMART Goal—

- Establish the SMART goal for the next unit of study. Please bring a unit plan from your next unit of study.

  - What is essential in the unit?

  - What do students have to be able to do?

  - How do we measure it and when?

  - What percentage will be proficient on the assessment?

  - For students not proficient, what is the essential skill that students will have and how is it measured?

  - When is the essential learning reassessed?

- Share your SMART goal.

Team Leader Self-Assessment:

- What are the areas in your team leader role in which you need to grow? (Kullar, 2018). Team leaders self-reflect on areas for growth. The follow-up activity is for each team leader to share the area they chose, the steps in the process, and the results of that plan. Areas that team leaders reflected on include the following.

  - I know and understand my role as a team leader.

  - I provide professional development opportunities for my team.

  - I communicate issues related to my team and propose solutions to the administration.

  - I model professional behavior by being positive and supportive of the administration.

  - I have critical conversations when needed with team members.

  - I take the initiative to resolve issues with my team.

  - I am always thinking of ways to improve my school.

  - I use conflict and mediation skills to ensure effective collaboration with my team.

  - I frequently analyze data as they pertain to my team and lead conversations for improvement.

  - I provide constructive and actionable feedback to my team.

- Team leaders rate themselves on each leadership factor as *consistently*, *usually*, *occasionally*, and *rarely*.

Source: White River School District, 2020. Used with permission.

Figure 2.5: Sample building leadership team meeting agenda aligned to district team leadership meeting learning.

Chapter 3

Leading the Work at the School Level: The Building Leadership Team

Authors Salleh Hairon and Clive Dimmock (2012) state, "Unquestionably, leadership and leader competence will play a large part in the success or otherwise with which PLCs are accepted, implemented, sustained and scaled up across the school system" (pp. 405–424). They are right. The critical building leadership team this chapter explores—the principal and teacher collaborative team leaders—advances the work of the district leadership team and helps to provide a sense of *systemness* at the building level. Richard DuFour and Michael Fullan (2013) define this term and provide an important reminder:

> Systemness—the degree to which people identify and are committed to an entity larger than themselves—is not about letting others work to get the system right so that you will be better off. It is about everyone doing their part in two aspects: being as good as one can be during individual and collaborative work, and being aware that everyone needs to make a contribution to improving the larger system. (p. 18)

Members of this team lead the work of a PLC at the school level. They practice and rehearse the work they expect of individual grade-level and content teams, anticipate questions from these teams, and share learning data. Essentially, the building leadership team members learn together and answer the four critical questions of a PLC before asking grade-level or content teams to engage in the work.

This chapter also focuses on how the building principal aligns his or her work with the teacher collaborative team leaders as they work together to improve the professional practice of staff to increase student learning for every team. When the principal is deeply engaged with the work of his or her team, they experience a greater commitment to the success of the entire school. These principals focus on the quality of instruction in their schools. As the Wallace Foundation (2013) notes, "They emphasize research-based strategies to improve teaching and learning and initiate discussions about instructional approaches, both in teams and with individual teachers" (p. 11).

In chapter 2 (page 49), we talked about the district leadership team meeting, in which district office staff, principals, and building learning coordinators learn together. In White River School District, district leaders ask that before leaving the meeting, each principal make a commitment to continue the work at his or her own school. Each principal has electronic access to all the resources from the district leadership team learning meeting, such as SMART goals, unit plans, learning targets and success criteria, evidence of progress, and so on. They are equipped and ready to do the work in their building, and of course district office administrators are always available and happy to provide any additional assistance.

In White River, the building leadership team includes the principal, assistant principal, building learning coordinator, team leaders (one per grade level, content-area team, or grade-level course, to include special education, Title I, English learner staff, and a school counselor). It is also important to include a member of the paraeducator team. Our para-educators join with the teacher collaborative teams to provide interventions on Tier 2 and 3 skills with students. Including them as active participants in the RTI/MTSS conversation makes it that much richer, as they are often aware of the specific Tier 3 skills that students lack. This team first practices the work it will expect of its school grade-level or content-area teams based on the commitment the principal set in his or her work on the district leadership team. As we shared in the introduction to this book in figure I.1 (page 10), this team performs the following functions.

- Collaboratively develop role definitions and shared commitments.
- Develop team norms and accountability protocols.
- Focus on learning.
- Meet regularly, and send out and follow agenda.
- Set improvement goals.
- Practice and rehearse the work of grade-level and content-area collaborative teams.
- Analyze student learning, seek best practice, and share findings.
- Monitor results using a continuous improvement cycle.
- Model the behavior expected of others.
- Celebrate improvement.

The principal and the collaborative team leaders work to create layers of leadership, participate in team leader training, lead the learning, establish clarity about the work, monitor team progress toward goals, build a healthy culture, and engage in cycles of collective inquiry.

Create Layers of Leadership

Often principals and teacher leaders have an idea of what leaders should be—how they should act, the goals they should have, and the image they project. However, when we as leaders think about the best boss we've ever had, that vision doesn't always mesh with the image of the leader we think we need to be. For example, many people think a good leader needs to be all knowing. If a staff member has a question, the leader should have the answer, right? This might seem ideal, but in reality, this idea of a strong leader is difficult to live up to daily. If as a leader, you think you need to have all the answers to all the questions, facing a question you don't know the answer to could cause a sense of panic—for you and potentially for the staff, if you have projected the image of being all knowing.

One of the three big ideas of a PLC is a collaborative culture (DuFour et al., 2016). When teachers collaborate, they are stronger, and they get better results for students than they do as individuals working in isolation. The same holds true at the leadership level. Each school in White River is expected to have a building leadership team that includes grade-level or content-area team leaders. Just like the building learning coordinator, team leaders must have a demonstrated record of effectiveness with student learning. To be successful, team leaders must be effective educators—educators who gets results with their students. They must have earned the recognition and respect of their peers. Eaker and Keating (2009) write:

> The quality of work performed by teams depends on team leaders who join with their principal to direct the team's work ensuring that the team is focusing on the right things and continually improving, laboring together to improve student learning. Just as district success depends on the leadership capability of superintendents and school success depends to a great degree on the leadership of principals, the success of collaborative teams depends on the leadership capacity of team leaders.

In their roles, team leaders should lead the work of their team, work closely with the building learning coordinator, and report directly to the building principal. They also serve as contributing members of the building leadership team. Michael D. Bayewitz and his coauthors (2020) explain, "Leaders should understand why this work is important and know how to help their teams when they have questions about the process" (p. 49).

Having layers of leadership provides a variety of benefits. Of course, the obvious benefit is creating leadership capacity in individual staff members. As Jim Collins (2001) puts it, principals should think about "getting the right people on the bus, the right people in the right seats, and the wrong people off the bus" (p. 41). Bringing teacher voices to the table only makes school leaders better. While principals typically start out as teachers, for many, it's been years since they've been in a classroom. Theory is great, but the practical voice of someone who is in the classroom daily and can talk about how to put theory into practice is important. And finally, there is no doubt that there are times when it is easier for teachers to be vulnerable, ask questions, and seek help from a peer rather than their evaluator, the principal. We would prefer that the answer comes from an exemplary teacher leader.

In White River, principals carefully select their team leaders. Not only do team leaders work with every teacher on his or her team but they also work closely with the principal. Team leaders are incredibly important to the success of a team. In particular, if a team includes new teachers, the team leader not only leads the work of the team but simultaneously shows new teachers how to do the work along with the norms of the school community. These new teachers are people who could potentially go on to have a thirty-year career in your building, so starting them on the right path matters.

The right team leader will exponentially leverage the work of the team. As it says in our team leader position description, team leaders are expected to enhance the capacity of their team to work interdependently to achieve common goals for which team members hold themselves mutually accountable. See figure 3.1 for the position description for a team leader in White River School District. In White River, we have learned that leaving the decision to the team to elect a leader or simply asking for volunteers does not usually produce the best leader. Traditional methods of selecting team leaders such as rotating people on a yearly basis, selecting the most senior member of the team, placing the newest member of the team in the position, or simply having the team choose a leader won't be successful in supporting growth and developing a high-performing team.

Team Leader Position Description

A high-performing collaborative team of teachers is the heart and soul of a school that functions as a PLC, and a highly effective team is invariably led by an effective team leader. The success of the White River School District to achieve its mission of ensuring high levels of learning for all students depends to a great degree on the leadership capacity of the team leaders in each school. Thus, the selection of team leaders in White River is a thoughtful, informed, and deliberate decision of critical importance.

The educators who serve in this very important role are expected to coordinate and lead the work of their teams. They will work closely with the learning improvement coordinator within their building and *report directly to the building principal.* Additionally, team leaders serve as contributing members of the principal's administrative team. Team leaders are expected to articulate and communicate to the administration any faculty questions, needs, and concerns, while at the same time communicating and explaining the rationale and specifics of the administration's plans and initiatives to the faculty. In short, the team leader serves as the *key communications link* between the administration and faculty.

Team leaders are expected to enhance the capacity of their teams to work *interdependently* to achieve *common* goals for which team members hold themselves *mutually accountable.* In fulfilling their role of leading their teams, team leaders are responsible for such functions as leading the team in preparing and utilizing team norms, planning agendas, chairing meetings, serving as a direct communications link between the administration and the faculty, leading the work of teams in analyzing and improving student learning data, seeking out and experimenting with best practices, leading the collaborative development and attainment of learning improvement goals, and identifying and communicating professional development needs. *Team leaders must work continually to enhance the effectiveness of their teams by ensuring that the team focuses on the critical questions and practices associated with improving student learning in a manner that reflects the highest quality.*

Educators who serve as team leaders must have a *demonstrated record of effectiveness in their own teaching* and they must have *earned the recognition and respect of their peers.* Team leaders must have excellent planning and organizational skills, as well as the ability to work well with others. In order to enhance the leadership capacity and effectiveness of others, team leaders must model a desire and willingness to continually learn, constantly seeking ways to first improve themselves so that they can more effectively lead their teams.

In short, the White River School District is seeking *outstanding* individuals to lead building-level collaborative teams of teachers in order to more effectively impact student leaning levels—student by student, skill by skill, relentlessly and continually!

Source: Eaker & Keating, 2009.

Figure 3.1: Collaborative team leader description.

Annually, the White River School District seeks outstanding individuals to lead building-level collaborative teams of teachers in order to more effectively impact student learning levels, student by student, skill by skill, relentlessly and continually. The position of team leader is a coveted and respected role in the district and at each school site. There's no formal application process. The principal simply invites teachers to indicate an interest in the role or nudges a teacher to come forward to be interviewed for the position. Any teacher interested will be interviewed. Principals use the tool in figure 3.2 to guide the selection of the team leaders.

Name of Candidate: Date:	
Oral and Written Communication Skills The team leader serves as the key communication link between the principal and the grade-level or content team.	**Evidence of Effective Communication Skills:**
Organizational Skills The team leader is responsible for such functions as leading the team in preparing and utilizing team norms and accountability protocols, agendas, leading the work of teams in analyzing and improving student learning data, planning interventions and extensions, seeking out and experimenting with best instructional practices, leading the collaborative development and attainment of SMART goals, and identifying and communicating professional development needs.	**Evidence of Effective Organization Skills:**
Effective in Professional Practice The team leader must have a demonstrated record of effectiveness in his or her own teaching. The team leaders must get results with student learning.	**Evidence of Effective Professional Practice:**
Ability to Positively Influence Peers The team leader must have a positive disposition toward his or her job, bring solutions to the table, work constantly to build the capacity of teammates, and have across-grade-level influence.	**Evidence of the Ability to Positively Influence Peers:**
Model a Desire and Willingness to Continually Learn The team leader must constantly be seeking ways to first improve his or her leadership skills and professional practice so that he or she can more effectively lead the team.	**Evidence of a Desire and Willingness to Continually Learn:**

Source: White River School District, 2019. Used with permission.

Figure 3.2: Collaborative team leader–selection tool.

*Visit **go.SolutionTree.com/PLCbooks** to download a free reproducible copy of this figure.*

Participate in Team Leader Training

Team leader training should be at the top of every principal's before-school-starts must-do list. This training is a foundational component for teams as it ensures success in the work collaborative teams will engage in throughout the school year. Just as principals provide training for teachers new to the district, they should also provide support and direction for teacher leaders who will be guiding the work of their grade-level or content-area collaborative teams.

At White River, the collaborative team leaders read chapter 9 of *Learning by Doing* (DuFour et al., 2016), "Addressing Conflict and Celebrating in a Professional Learning Community," annually. Each team leader is expected to support, guide, and *lead* his or her team. As DuFour and Fullan (2013) point out:

> A strong leadership team, or a guiding coalition, with shared objectives is essential in the early stages of any organization's improvement process. . . . Every large-scale success that we have been associated with has been led by people who saw that their main lever for change was to create ever-expanding circles of leaders focused on whole-system reform: leaders developing other leaders with focus. (p. 24)

Principal Mothershead spoke about the importance of collaborative team leader training for the 2019–2020 school year (the school's fourteenth year of implementation) this way:

> We revisited the district focus areas and our data to plan for the work ahead. The majority of the meeting was to provide clarity of the role of the leadership team, the expectation of the focus on learning, using data, and providing tools for team leaders to have crucial conversations with team members when appropriate. (C. Mothershead, personal communication, September 9, 2019)

Figure 3.3 is a continuum used during team leader training to assess the school's current reality. Figure 3.4 (page 81) is a secondary team leader training agenda used in middle and high schools in White River School District.

After many years of doing individual school collaborative team leader trainings, the principals decided to conduct training together for all the elementary principals and collaborative team leaders. The benefit of such an approach is that principals and team leaders are consistent in their learning and planning across the district, sending a common message to each team in every school by speaking with the same voice and truly meaning it when they say, "These are all of our kids." The role and responsibilities of team leaders are consistent across each grade level and the various buildings, which enhances the systemness we previously described. The training meeting also served to calibrate the group's thinking and establish common expectations for all teams. The agenda for the elementary meeting appears in figure 3.5 (page 81).

Indicator	Pre-initiating	Initiating	Implementing	Developing	Sustaining
Sense of Purpose	Team consists of administrators only. Information flows top down. Policies and procedures are primary discussion topics.	Attempt to create a building leadership team, but there is not a clear sense of purpose. Team members assigned based on seniority or popular vote by team. There is no clarity on how this team will have an impact on learning.	A team leader position description and statement of purpose for the team exists. The building leadership team has established collective commitments and improvement goals. There is an annual training, but there is little transfer of knowledge and information from the building learning coordinator back to team members.	There is a clearly defined sense of purpose for the building leadership team, which is to improve learning for all students in the school. Building staff view the building leadership team as the decision-making body for the school. The team learns together and begins to see themselves as the key for school improvement. Annual training supports the needs of the team based on the school's achievement data.	The building learning team is highly engaged in the work of improving learning. Annual training supports members, leadership needs, buildingwide focus areas, and how to use data effectively to improve learning.
Collective Efficacy	The staff feel that they do not have input on important decisions that affect them.	Teacher leaders may not view the shared leadership connections as important to their collective success.	The building leadership team begins to see the value in having common language, expectations, and outcomes in all classrooms.	A sense of collective efficacy emerges and can be observed in common practices such as selecting essential standards, unit planning, intervention, and extension. Feedback and reporting of student progress toward meeting essential standards (grading).	The building learning team shares best practices and problem solves together. Important decisions that require staff commitment are discussed and agreed on annually, to include selecting essential standards, unit planning, intervention, and extension. The team comes to consensus on feedback and reporting of student progress toward meeting essential standards (grading). The master schedule reflects a focus on learning; Tier 1, 2, and 3 instruction is visible in the master schedule. Social-emotional learning for students is implemented consistently throughout the district.

continued ▲

Figure 3.3: Team leader training current reality assessment tool.

Impact on Learning	There is little observable impact that this meeting will have on learning other than compliance to schoolwide policies and procedures.	The building leadership team has an annual training, but the agenda reflects "nuts and bolts" rather than a focus on learning.	The building leadership team engages in reviewing district focus areas, school learning data, and other important topics, but there is not a sense of urgency to set priorities or expect improvement.	The building leadership team engages in an annual training that supports the work to the team leaders and leads the team to the understanding that their purpose is to lead the work of improving learning for all students in the school.	The building leadership team is deeply engaged in learning leadership strategies and effective communication strategies. They monitor academic and behavior data for the purpose of determining next steps for a grade level or the entire school. Social-emotional learning data is reviewed for the purpose of creating supports where necessary.
Districtwide Process	Annual building leadership team training is not required and is not consistent across schools. The agenda is left up to the individual principal to determine.	The building leadership team has an annual training, but there is no connection between the agenda from the district leadership team administrative retreat and the building leadership team annual training.	The building leadership team has an annual training connected to the district leadership team administrative retreat agenda, but there is not a sense of urgency to set priorities or expect improvement.	Building leadership team annual training begins to develop similar expectations and outcomes in all buildings in the district. Grade-level team leaders from across the district meet together, creating the sense that "these kids are our kids."	There is a direct connection between the district leadership team training and the building leadership team training each year. Building leadership teams from each level, elementary through secondary, meet regularly throughout the year to ensure that practices are common across the district.
Leadership Building Capacity	There is no opportunity for teacher team leaders to build leadership capacity.	Teacher team leaders begin to build leadership capacity, but it is dependent on the quality of the principal leadership.	Teacher team leaders are asked to lead professional development on effective instructional strategies and data analysis, and with their school-level teams.	Teacher team leaders learn from each other throughout the district and are often called on to highlight the work of their teacher teams with the district leadership team and school board.	Teacher leaders gain experience and knowledge that supports their professional growth. Collaborative team leaders may move into the building leadership team role, instructional coaches, and TOSAs, and are supported in pursuing their administrative credentials.

Source: White River School District, 2020. Used with permission.

Secondary Team Leader Training Agenda

1. Begin with an opening activity.

2. Establish norms and accountability protocols.

3. Review the organizational purpose of the principal and collaborative team leaders.

4. Incorporate critical information from the district administrative retreat (for example, a focus on lesson design or effective communication strategies).

5. Review priorities from the previous year and establish priorities for the current year.

   - Review pertinent data.

   - Review Tier 2 and Tier 3 intervention expectations.

6. Set schoolwide SMART goals.

7. Review team leader expectations.

   - Review position description.

   - Review tips for crucial conversations (chapter 9 in *Learning by Doing* [DuFour et al., 2016]).

   - Review and practice dysfunctional team scenarios.

8. Review weekly collaborative meeting expectations.

   - Read and discuss "Stomping Out PLC Lite" (Keating & Rhoades, 2019).

   - Review relevant student learning data or student work.

   - Use the schoolwide PLC planner.

Figure 3.4: Secondary team leader training agenda.

Elementary Team Leader Training Agenda

Review roles and expectations of the team leader.

- Set norms and accountability protocols.

- Review products to be generated as a result of collaborative time.

- Update the PLC planner.

- Establish and track SMART goals unit by unit.

- Send Friday reminders to the collaborative team regarding teamwork in the Monday morning meeting.

- Commit to closing every meeting by asking, "What did we agree to? What evidence will we bring to our next meeting?"

Figure 3.5: Elementary team leader training agenda.

Messages from White River's principals speak to the power of this leader training and how it impacts the work of collaborative teams. Janel Ross, assistant principal at the White River Early Learning Center, made the following comments:

> The great part about having the districtwide leadership team meet and learn together is they all hear the same message. This will be especially important since collaboration at the Early Learning Center will include members from multiple schools on a weekly basis. Because we met all together in August, there was clarity on expectations across the board. (J. Ross, personal communication, August 19, 2019)

Laurie Gelinas, the principal of Wilkeson Elementary School, stated:

> Our districtwide leadership team meeting gave our teacher leaders an opportunity to revisit the purpose of collaboration meetings, discuss obstacles, and define our essential next steps to collectively improve learning. I am grateful to work in a district where there is such a high level of support for one another. (L. Gelinas, personal communication, August 19, 2019)

Jeff Byrnes, the principal of Mountain Meadow Elementary School, addressed his staff when he said:

> We are not adding more; we need to keep getting better at what we do. What do you need to stop doing, because we are going to continue to get better at what we do daily? I think at the beginning of the year, we talked about going slow to go fast. Let's make sure everyone is very aware of the expectations of our grade-level teams, instruction, interventions, and assessment. We have new teams, new team leads, we need everyone on the same page and then we can pick up the pace to increase student learning. (J. Byrnes, personal communication, August 19, 2019)

Mark Cushman, the principal of Foothills Elementary School, summed up the significance of the event by addressing the group at the end of the meeting. He said:

> In all my years working with team leaders in our district, I have never seen all of the instructional leaders in our elementary schools assembled in one room. Make no mistake, each of you has been selected as a team leader because you are master teachers—difference-makers, if you will. To all be here, hearing the same message, establishing shared norms, as well as a shared vision of where we want to go not just as individual schools, but collectively as the elementary instructional leaders in our district, is amazing. I believe we are on the verge of demonstrating the true power of collective efficacy. We are all in this together, and I want to thank you for choosing to be a part of the White River Elementary leadership team. There is no limit to what we are going to accomplish. This will be an amazing year! (M. Cushman, personal communication, August 19, 2019)

Lead the Learning

The principal and collaborative team leaders lead the learning in the school. The team does this through regular monthly meetings. Annually, the team creates norms and accountability protocols. The members practice and rehearse new learning that the principal developed and practiced within the district leadership team meetings. These monthly meetings provide an opportunity to explore points of confusion, answer questions, and really work out the kinks before sharing processes and procedures with individual grade-level or content-area teams and the entire staff. Along with new learning, this team spends time reviewing unit plans, SMART goals, and unit assessment data. The intent is not to say, "Gotcha!" to collaborative teams that may not have gotten strong results, but rather to help build and share best instructional practices by learning what individual collaborative teams are doing and checking in on student learning across the school. These meetings can also be a place to get peer input when a team leader is working with a struggling team or team member. Often, struggles one team is facing are the same as those that other teams have already experienced, and their insights can be helpful. The team must have a definite "these kids are our kids" attitude. Its primary purpose is to improve learning for all students and staff in the district.

Establish Clarity About the Work

As the principal and collaborative team leaders work together to improve learning, it is critical that each team leader sees how all the collaborative work fits together. Principal Mothershead did not assume that all his team leaders, and therefore teams, internalized how all the work of improving learning was connected. He did not leave it to chance. At a building leadership team meeting, he organized team leaders into groups of three. He then handed each group an envelope and a piece of poster paper. The envelope contained strips of paper labeled individually with learning components. Each piece included words such as *standard, learning target, SMART goal, formative assessment, success criteria*, and *additional time and support*. All labeled strips represented the work teams undertake around the four critical questions of a PLC: (1) what is it we want students to know and be able to do? (2) how will we know if each student has learned it? (3) how will we respond when some student do learn it? and (4) how will we extend the learning for students who have demonstrated proficiency? (DuFour et al., 2016). He asked each team to use the poster paper to create a diagram that showed how all the words on the individual strips of paper were connected. This process produced a number of *a-ha* moments as teams shared their diagrams recreating what we fondly refer to as the *repeating process* (see figure 3.6, page 84).

By completing this activity, the teams realized that each of the component in the repeating process is not a stand-alone item. Each connects directly to the daily lesson and to the unit. For example, the entry task, daily instructional strategy, and the exit task are connected back to the daily learning target and serve as launching points for students to access prior knowledge. This highlighted the critical importance of attaching instructional strategies directly to the learning target.

It is the building leadership team's responsibility to ensure learning for all students in the school. Each team leader will take his or her learning to his or her grade-level or content-area team and walk through it again with his or her team members. It is important for this team to have clarity about the work, see the connectedness, and model the work expected for each team in the building. This team learns together and the members hold each other accountable for high-quality products and evidence of learning. It also provides support and direction for team leaders, allowing them to grow in their leadership, as well as ensure common learning expectations across all teams in the building.

The Repeating Process in White River School District

1. Establish a SMART goal.

2. Identify essential standards and unwrap standards into learning targets. Develop proficiency scales or success criteria.

3. Create an end-of-unit formative assessment.

4. Design instruction and engagement activities connected to the individual learning target and success criteria.

5. Design checks for understanding aligned with learning targets and provide feedback to students.

6. Provide additional time and support aligned to the target, check for understanding, and provide feedback to students.

7. Weekly, come to the team meeting prepared to discuss what students have learned based on the check for understanding (data or student work).

8. At the end of the unit, discuss the conditions to give the assessment, then distribute the assessment.

9. Score and analyze the assessment.

10. Reflect using the TACA form (see chapter 1, page 25).

11. Look at data and student work.

12. Apply interventions and extensions.

13. Review SMART goal.

14. Repeat the process in the next unit.

Figure 3.6: The repeating process for each unit in White River School District.

Monitor Team Progress Toward Goals

The building leadership team meets monthly to review end-of-unit common formative assessment data. The team leaders come equipped to share information from their grade-level or content-area team TACA. Grade level by grade level, they share their data, student work, and effective instructional strategies. Teams now have the data to validate that specific instructional strategies work with students. Teams also share where students struggled in the unit. This building leadership team meeting is a powerful vertical team meeting. For example, if a third-grade team is sharing where students struggled, the second-grade team leader can note to make some instructional adjustments in that unit in second grade. The fourth-grade team leader should be making note that these students likely will need some support with the prerequisite skills when they enter fourth grade. If they are examining an end-of-year standard, the entire building leadership team will brainstorm strategies to help the third-grade students meet the standard by the end of third grade.

In ELA, White River grade-level teams work on the same standards at the same time of the year. For example, in September every third-grade team works on 3.RLI.1: Ask and answer questions to demonstrate understanding of a text, referring explicitly to the text as the basis for the answers. At the end of the unit, grade-level team leaders come to the meeting armed with examples of proficient student work. The leadership team will then post the student work beginning with kindergarten and see the vertical progression of that standard up through fifth grade.

At the secondary level, you will observe the principal and leadership team examining data from singleton CTE teachers. Each CTE teacher has agreed to collect data on how his or her students are doing on a specific skill. You will also observe the teams reviewing data from a specific course to include ninth-grade ELA or algebra. The TACA process drives the conversation. For example, the algebra team leader would start by sharing the SMART goal for unit 1: 85 percent of students will be proficient or higher on the end-of-unit assessment on solving multistep linear equations. All students will be able to solve an algebraic two-step equation. The team leader then shares where students did well and where students struggled. The course-by-course data is archived and the team leader notes how the current algebra students did in comparison to previous years. This is an important discussion as it's tied to decisions the team made during Tier 1 instruction and Tier 2 interventions.

The building leadership team also spends time examining what's actually being written and recorded in the TACA. For example, there's a section that requires the team to write down what Tier 2 interventions were provided in the unit, target by target. If the team simply writes down that the students received small-group instruction, that is not enough detail. The team needs to write down which instructional strategies and resources they used during the Tier 2 intervention. Keep in mind the TACA process is a process for teams to talk about their students, their learning, and about the instructional strategies that helped students learn grade-level standards. It's the continuous improvement cycle in action. If there's not enough detail in the TACA form, the team leaders will ensure that as they use the TACA on the next unit, the grade-level or content-area team adds useful detail to each section.

All teams are expected to write SMART goals for each unit of instruction throughout the school year. It is the responsibility of the building leadership team to monitor each team's progress toward meeting its goals. Goal setting provides clarity on what teams expect students to learn by clearly articulating what is essential in the unit. DuFour and his coauthors (2016) state, "In short, there is *nothing* more important in determining the effectiveness of a team than each member's understanding of and commitment to the achievement of results-oriented goals to which the group holds itself mutually accountable" (p. 103).

The building leadership team reviews student learning data from the previous year, establishes goals for the upcoming year, and also engages in professional development for the purpose of meeting those goals. Professional development opportunities could include training with mathematics and ELA TOSAs or content-area specialists. The professional development is specifically tied to instructional strategies that will advance the work of the standards unit by unit. For example, the student learning data from the previous year might indicate that a team will need professional development on close-reading strategies, text-dependent questions, or effective vocabulary instruction.

Build a Healthy Culture

To create a healthy school culture, building principals must begin by understanding the school environment. Muhammad and Cruz (2019) are succinct when they state:

> To intentionally create environments conducive to adult learning, transformational leaders must lead by example and embrace becoming lifelong learners themselves. In schools we visit as consultants, we note a distinction between leaders who continuously invest in learning with other members of their organization and those who do not. (p.122)

A healthy culture must also be built on trust. Trust isn't something you can create through initiatives. Trust can't be established with a single event. Trust has to be built over time by aligning words and actions—not once, but over and over again.

School culture can be loosely defined by the sum total of all the attitudes, opinions, and behaviors of the team members. When principals and team leaders clarify and support the expectations of a collaborative team, and team members engage in the work, trust is built and school culture improves.

In White River, the building learning coordinator can be an effective resource when working to build trust and ensure all voices are heard. You will hear how important it is to select the right person for the role, as Katie Vail, Foothills Elementary building learning coordinator, shares:

> The role of a building learning coordinator is more comprehensive than that of a team leader. In this role, it's important to communicate and connect with each team to make sure that the voices of your staff are being heard. Your team is now every grade-level team in your building. You are the main messenger between the principal and the staff. Being this teacher leader means that your staff is comfortable sharing with you their true thoughts and feelings about the decisions made at the district leadership team and building leadership team meetings. These informal conversations can provide your principal with the insight that is needed to make decisions that are beneficial for all stakeholders. Your principal expects you to share the views of teachers and give them (your principal) a perspective they don't have. You also serve as a conduit for cross-grade-level communication, which doesn't happen as often during weekly collaboration meetings.
>
> In addition to being a critical communicator, you serve as a leader for your school leadership team. The meetings and discussions that you have as a building leadership team are facilitated and planned by you in conjunction with your principal. You have the unique knowledge and capacity to share the messages from the district leadership team meetings, and help your school align with the vision that comes from those. During this time, collaboration is very powerful. The discussions you facilitate and decisions members make during this meeting have input from each unique situation in the school. As a building learning coordinator, you can capture that thinking and foster productive solution-oriented conversations. Your role allows you to make sure there is alignment between grade levels and that important stakeholders accept and share decisions in your building. (K. Vail, personal communication, September 4, 2020)

There are a number of ways that the principal and collaborative team leaders can aid in building trust, addressing conflict, and ensuring that all stakeholders have a voice. It starts with selecting the right team leaders. The team leader position description in figure 3.2 (page 77) can serve as a guide for the principal when making this important decision. Once the team leaders have been selected, the building leadership team must accomplish the following work, and collaborative team leaders must do the same with their grade-level or content-area teams.

- Write their norms and accountability protocols
- Read chapter 9 in *Learning by Doing* (DuFour et al., 2016), "Addressing Conflict and Celebrating in a Professional Learning Community"

Trust is built through clear communication and expectations and engaging in the right work—"Work that is designed to require people to act in new ways creates the possibility of new experiences. These new experiences, in turn, can lead to new attitudes over time" (DuFour et al, 2016, p. 220).

This work creates avenues to critical discussions that encourage different viewpoints about how the team will function in an effort to reach its goals. Respectful dialogue and discourse should be the norm. High-performing leadership teams are more than a collection of individuals who meet together; they have agreed-on ways of doing things and members make commitments to each other regarding how they will work together day in and day out to ensure high levels of learning for each student and support each other in this mission. Teams agree to use norms and accountability protocols to govern themselves.

As teacher collaborative teams take responsibility for the learning of all students in their grade level or course, they naturally become more accountable to each other for ensuring learning for all students they serve. What does it mean to take responsibility for student learning? It starts with coming to the collaborative team meeting prepared. Team members commit to arriving armed with data or student work that represents what standard or specific learning target was essential that week. That single move goes a long way toward building trust. As a team member, it sends the message, "I care about improving our professional practice and improving student learning." When team members are stressed or worried that data will be used against them or an honest reflective comment will be tagged as negative, there's really nothing a principal or team leader can say that will get them to believe; actions are important, not words. When the team members experience the principal and team leader reflecting, guiding, and being solution and action oriented, they are establishing a trusting relationship and creating a healthy culture by doing the work of a collaborative team. Muhammad and Cruz (2019) reinforce this powerful belief by stating:

> While teacher leaders continuously hone their craft due to the fact that they are still teachers, they can lead by example by continuously strengthening their ability to couple their teaching with evidence of learning, and then share their experience and findings with fellow teachers. (p. 122)

The principal has a vital role in building a healthy culture. It's important the principal be present at teacher collaborative team meetings to listen and support members' work. Being present allows the principal to understand the problems the team is grappling with and the guidance that the team may need to move forward. The principal can provide clarity when necessary, communicating the why and providing the rationale for decisions the team makes. When a principal is willing to pull up a chair and support the work of a team, it goes a long way toward building trust and sending the message that the work of the collaborative team matters.

In addition, the principal has the responsibility for advocating for and providing a team with training or support if needed. The principal is ultimately responsible for ensuring that norms are adhered to, and that team members are coming to the table prepared. If that doesn't happen, it erodes the team trust and sends the message that this is not important. Vitally, principals need to see a teacher's class data as a place for reciprocal accountability. If a teacher cannot count on the principal to give him or her support when and where it is needed, being transparent with data becomes a painful process. Reciprocal accountability builds trust. Trust builds a healthy school culture.

Engage in Cycles of Collective Inquiry and Action Research

DuFour and his coauthors (2016) state that for teams to become high performing they must engage in recurring cycles of collective inquiry and action research to achieve better results for students. Austin Buffum, Mike Mattos, and Janet Malone (2018) emphasize:

> It is essential for the team to embrace the importance of doing the work, not just leading the work. In other words, team members must establish and live a culture of collective responsibility among themselves in order to model, inform, and establish a similar culture in the school as a whole. (p. 40)

In the following sections, we explore examples of the collaborative work the principal and collaborative team leaders do in White River schools.

Unwrapping Standards

One example of the work of the principal and content team leaders is the collaborative task of unwrapping standards into learning targets. This is the process grade-level and content-area teams use to bring clarity to the essential learning in a unit. By the time the principal and building learning coordinator lead the work for all staff, with the support of their leadership team, they have already had at least two interactions with the process: (1) at the district level and (2) again at the school level with collaborative team leaders. The goal, of course, is that every educator in the system will understand how to unwrap an essential standard into clear learning targets. Furthermore, leaders should strive to ensure that every teacher is clear on the purpose of a learning target—to drive instruction and learning, check for understanding, give feedback, and indicate when to provide additional time, support, and extension. This work has a systemwide impact.

For example, our high school English team used Kim Bailey, Chris Jakicic, and Jeanne Spiller's (2014) book *Collaborating for Success With the Common Core* as a resource to guide the work surrounding unwrapping standards. Tracy Nelson, an English language arts TOSA, was also a valuable team resource with the unwrapping process (see figure 3.7).

RL.3.1: Ask and answer questions to demonstrate an understanding of a text, referring explicitly to the text as the basis for the answers.

Knowledge Targets

- Students must know that details and examples from literary text can be used as textual evidence to support an answer.

- Students must know that explicit references are based on exactly what is written in literary text.

Reasoning Targets

- Students must ask questions about literary text referring to specific details.

- Students must answer questions about a literary text using explicit references to support their answers.

- Students must find evidence within a literary text to support an answer.

- Students must refer to text to support their conclusions.

Source for standard: NGA & CCSSO, 2010a.

Figure 3.7: Unwrapping an essential reading literature standard for third grade.

Setting SMART Goals

In the second example (see figure 3.8), the team focused on SMART goals. The SMART goal is tied to an essential standard, or a target or skill within an essential standard. Creating meaningful SMART goals for each unit of instruction is another example of systemness in action. After getting some practice in creating SMART goals in the district leadership team meeting, the principals and building learning coordinator take the process to the principal and collaborative team leaders, and they work to build shared knowledge. They then dig in and practice writing a goal for their next unit of instruction. As a team, they come to a consensus regarding the expectations and purpose of SMART goals for each team in the school. Now each team leader is equipped to write a SMART goal with his or her grade-level or content-area team for the next unit of instruction. Most importantly, they agree on when to check on results toward achieving the SMART goal, unit by unit. It is unreasonable to think that a school will meet its overall SMART goals if a team doesn't meet its unit-by-unit SMART goals.

By the end of Unit 1—September 27—100 percent of students will be able to solve for the volume of a regular rectangular prism using the formula L x W x H, or B x H as measured by questions 7a and 7b on the end-of-unit assessment, and a level 3 on the proficiency scale.

Figure 3.8: Fourth-grade mathematics SMART goal.

Figure 3.9 highlights where the SMART goal fits into each unit. The SMART goal is based on an essential standard or a target of skill within an essential standard and measured by an end-of-unit assessment. The learning targets are deconstructed chunks of the essential standards. Quick formative assessments check the learning along the way, target by target. Teachers provide additional time, support, and extension based on the results of these quick formative assessments. Essentially, school grade-level and content-area teams focus what they teach on the targets, checking for understanding and providing additional time, support, and extension throughout the unit in an effort to meet the SMART goal. There should be no surprises on the end-of-unit assessment.

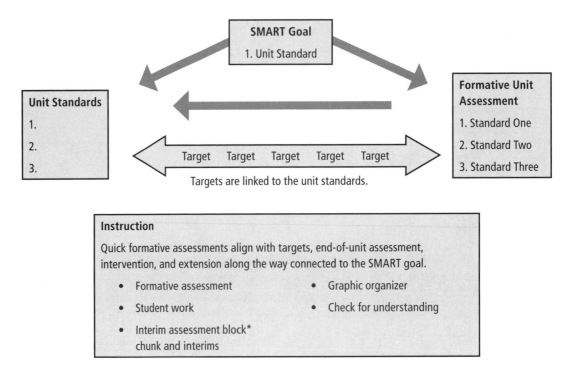

*Provided by Washington State as practice blocks for the required state assessment.

Figure 3.9: Systematic connections in a unit plan.

Conclusion

School improvement does not begin in the state capital in a legislative session or in the office of public instruction. It starts in every district with the creation of the conditions—layers of leadership opportunities—that develop and support teacher leaders. You already have everything you need. We promise you, this is the best hope for the daily change necessary in schools and public education in general. The next chapter will highlight just what teams do to improve learning for all students in their collaborative grade-level and content-area teams. This chapter is loaded with resources that every team can use, districtwide.

Chapter 4

Improving the Learning: Teacher Collaborative Teams

As DuFour and his coauthors (2016) note:

> Building a collaborative culture is simply a means to an end, not the end itself. The purpose of collaboration—to help more students achieve at higher levels—can only be accomplished if the professionals engaged in collaboration are focused on the right work. (p. 59)

So simply organizing educators into collaborative teams will have little or no effect on student learning unless teams are collaborating on the work that will increase student learning and school leaders are supporting them in doing so. Teams will require time, training, resources, and examples of best practice to do this right work.

In previous chapters, we highlighted that the right work of teacher teams in a PLC and in the White River School district is organized around the four critical questions of a PLC (DuFour et al., 2016). By answering these questions, teams work within a cycle of continuous improvement to collaboratively implement PLC processes and

create specific artifacts that yield evidence of their effectiveness.

1. **What do we want students to know and be able to do?** Clarifying what all students should learn in every subject, in every grade, in every course, in every unit, involves deep collaboration to determine essential standards (unit by unit at the elementary level and course by course at the secondary level). It requires setting SMART goals unit by unit, identifying learning targets, creating yearlong scope and sequence pacing, identifying success criteria in student work and developing proficiency scales, and providing Tier 1 core instruction, intervention, extension, and a unit plan to house the work layered under each of the four critical questions, along with instructional and engagement strategies.

2. **How will we know if each student has learned it?** To answer this question, teams must understand the assessment

process and the purpose of each assessment type, and collect student data, using, for example:

- Benchmark assessments—External measures designed to identify students who are ready to interact with grade-level standards, students in need of support, and students at risk

- Preassessments—Checks for prerequisite skills or the end-of-unit assessments used as the preassessment to measure growth

- Common formative end-of-unit assessments—Assessments to measure growth on essential standards in the unit

- Common formative team-generated checks for understanding—Checks that guide daily and weekly Tier 2 intervention plans based on specific learning targets (like entry tasks and exit slips)

- Performance tasks in which students demonstrate their mastery

- Interim assessment blocks from the state—Assessments (such as Smarter Balanced) that provide an external check on mastery of essential standards

- State assessments—Summative, moment-in-time assessments useful to identify program or classroom-level issues or weak areas in the curriculum

- Essential standards tracking chart—To track progress kid by kid and skill by skill

- Team Analysis of Common Assessment data-analysis protocol

3. **How will we respond if some students do not learn it?** Since PLCs recognize that students learn at different rates and in different ways, each school in White River School District develops a systematic plan to provide students with additional time and support if they struggle with the learning. To answer this question, school leaders create a master schedule that provides blocks of time for Tier 2 intervention and Tier 3 remediation of multiyear skill gaps, as well as blocks of time for Tier 2 and Tier 3 behavior intervention. Ensuring there is a master schedule in place that reflects the work of a team in a PLC is the responsibility of the principal who should seek input from every team. Collaborative teams plan interventions that address individual students, skill by skill, within the blocks of time in the master schedule. Tier 2 support is focused on very specific essential standards and learning targets. Tier 3 support is a block of time for students who require intensive intervention in foundational skills.

4. **How will we extend the learning for students who have demonstrated proficiency?** To extend the learning of students who demonstrate proficiency, collaborative teams use differentiated instruction (extensions they address in the unit plans, kid by kid).

In this chapter, we focus on what effective grade-level, content-area, and other types of collaborative teacher teams do and how district and building leadership provide the necessary support and reciprocal accountability for team success. Before collaborative teacher teams can focus on the right work involved in answering these four critical questions, however, they must understand that teams within PLCs need to focus on variables within their control.

Focus on Controllable Variables

Using collaborative time in a way that truly has an impact on student learning and educators' professional practice means staying focused on the *controllable variables*—those things teamwork can impact. If team members instead spend their collaborative time focusing on uncontrollable variables—such as by complaining about students, parents, the principal, and the district office—there will be no improvement in student learning. In fact, the time they spend collaborating will be wasted, along with district resources. Some teams slip into the pitfalls of the blame game and spend numerous hours debating the potential "what ifs" and "yeah buts" that get in the way of taking any responsibility for improving student learning. The more time they spend thinking about all the uncontrollable variables, the less time team members spend thinking about their controllable areas of influence. At White River, team effort and energy focus on the controllable variables (see figure 4.1).

Uncontrollable Variables	Controllable Variables
• Students can't pick their parents. • Students can't pick where they live. • Students can't pick the school they attend. • Students can't pick their teachers. • Students can't pick the high-stakes summative assessments.	• Culture of collaboration • Caring and encouraging classroom environment • Guaranteed and viable curriculum • Effective, research-based instructional strategies • Frequent monitoring and analysis of student learning • Additional time, support, and extension for learning • Frequent recognition and celebration of improvement

Source: © Eaker & Keating, 2010.

Figure 4.1: Uncontrollable and controllable variables.

As figure 4.1 shows, there are many variables that a grade-level or content-area team alone cannot impact. So in White River, grade-level and content teams focus their collaborative time on impacting the variables they can control. This chapter focuses on the work collaborative teams do to impact controllable variables.

- Create a caring and encouraging classroom.
- Build a guaranteed and viable curriculum.
- Determine SMART goals.
- Use effective, research-based, and affirmed instructional strategies.
- Frequently monitor and analyze evidence of student learning.
- Give timely feedback on student work.

- Provide additional time, support, and extension for learning.
- Frequently recognize and celebrate accomplishments.

Create a Caring and Encouraging Classroom Environment

Collaborative teams at White River work to create a culture of caring and encouragement in their classrooms. Teachers greet students at the door and are visible and present in the hallways. Students learn common expectations, and teachers get to know each student by creating a learning profile, student by student and class by class. Consider the work of Glacier Middle School, which is based on Greg Wolcott's (2019) *Significant 72: Unleashing the Power of Relationships in Today's Schools.*

Teacher teams carefully orchestrate the first three days—seventy-two hours—of school so that every student gets the same message, participating in the same activities to build relationships with teachers and with each other. By day four, when teachers begin teaching academics, they have set the stage for positive interactions and engagement. Researcher John Hattie (2009) identifies positive teacher-student relationships as significant, capable of producing nearly two years' student growth in one year's time. Hattie (as cited in Drive Learning, n.d.) shares:

> The positive teacher-student relationship is thus important not so much because this is worthwhile in itself, but because it helps build the trust to make mistakes, to ask for help, to build confidence to try again, and for students to know they will not look silly when they don't get it the first time.

But building relationships by itself is not enough. As Anthony Muhammad (2019) reminds us, "Love is not going to keep them out of prison or keep them out of the pitfalls of society because they don't have good skills." White River School District teams know that building relationships with students needs to be coupled with a guaranteed and viable curriculum.

Build a Guaranteed and Viable Curriculum

The greatest equity issue in American public education is the lack of a guaranteed and viable curriculum. A student's address in your district should not determine what he or she learns; the second grade should be second grade and include the same essential standards and same high-quality, rigorous end-of-unit assessments despite what walls surround it. The team is in control of what happens between essential standards and assessments. Stacey M. Childress, Denis P. Doyle, and David A. Thomas (2009) emphasize that "implementing a strategy of common, rigorous standards with differentiated resources and instruction can create excellence and equity for all students" (p. 133).

Collaborative teams in White River understand that *guaranteed and viable* means the essential standards in the unit need to be paced in a way that's doable for the teacher to teach and for the students to learn within the time available. In the White River system, the scope and sequence is the same across the district: teams have a tremendous amount of freedom within the timeframe highlighted in the unit plan skeleton and their blocked time in the master schedule to make decisions based on the learning needs of their students. Collaborative teams are aware that they will measure student learning of each of the identified essential standards by end-of-unit common formative assessments. If a student moves across town and attends a new school in the district, he or she will slide into the same unit of instruction addressing the same essential standards and will be assessed by the same common formative end-of-unit assessment. Establishing a guaranteed and viable curriculum is another controllable variable.

People often ask us, "How does a district that only has one school and one principal establish a guaranteed and viable curriculum without district support because *they are the district*?" Here's a place to start. Begin with one content area. In an elementary school, for example, ask each team to determine what's essential in mathematics. Teams would reference their state standards, the test map or blueprint, and their own knowledge and experience as teachers at their grade level. The principal would then need to make time for the third-grade team to meet with the fourth-grade team, giving its members an opportunity to ask this question: "If our students mastered these essential standards in third grade, would they be ready for the next level of learning in fourth grade?" The fourth-grade teacher team would have the opportunity to weigh in about what's essential in third grade. Both third- and fourth-grade teachers now have ownership of the third-grade standards. Can you see how this work can happen at all grade levels—kindergarten to first, first to second, continuing until a school has established essential standards at each grade level and content area?

It's impossible to do the work of a PLC if a team hasn't established essential standards. Think about this: what are teams assessing if they don't know what's essential? What are teams giving additional time and support on if they don't know what's most essential for students to learn?

To build a guaranteed and viable curriculum, teams center their conversations around the sequence of the essential standards. If the district leadership asks every school in the district to do the same work—determine and sequence essential standards—then this work is aligned districtwide. The district will then look for patterns that emerge in the work—school by school and team by team—and begin the process to determine essential standards districtwide. (We shared details of this process in chapter 1, page 13.)

Determine SMART Goals

Thankfully, our White River grade-level and content-area teacher collaborative teams have moved beyond writing SMART goals for compliance purposes. The days when the purpose was to write a SMART goal and turn it in with no expectation of follow-up are behind us. For White River teams, the purpose of the SMART goal is to bring clarity to exactly what team members expect students to learn in the unit of study. The SMART goal also drives what concepts and skills teams will be giving additional time and support on.

We've observed teams analyzing their data, making decisions about intervention groups, and working to ensure that the intervention will closely align to skills in their SMART goals. Notice in figure 4.2 that many SMART goals at White River have two parts. You will often see SMART goals written to say, for example, 80 percent of students will be able to meet this goal. But what is the expectation, then, for the remaining 20 percent of students? These students need to continue learning specific targets connected to the standard identified in the SMART goal. At White River, teachers may define a goal of less than 100 percent of students, but they need to write out what the next steps will be for students who didn't meet that goal.

First-Grade SMART Goals
Mathematics SMART Goals
Unit 3 goal: By the end of unit 3, 90 percent of our students will be able to add and subtract decimal numbers to the hundredths (5.NBT.7) as measured by a teacher-created common formative assessment. The remaining 10 percent will be able to add and subtract decimal numbers to the tenths as measured by a teacher-created common formative assessment.
Results: 85 percent of students demonstrated mastery of adding and subtracting decimals as measured by common formative assessment. Seventeen students did not show mastery of this standard. Seven students made a computational error in their work, but are demonstrating an ability to add and subtract with regrouping. The following students did not show an understanding of regrouping decimals when adding and/or subtracting: Corbin, Rylie S., Levon, Avalon, Mason, Emery, and Krisha.
Next steps: The students listed above will receive additional time and support as we begin to use the standard algorithm of multiplication and partial products when dividing. This will allow students daily practice with these skills with whole numbers and will allow them to develop an understanding of regrouping to apply it to decimals. These students will receive interventions during math club three days a week and then retake the formative assessment.
Final results: Eight of the remaining ten students were able to master the standard in the teacher-created formative assessment. The other two students will continue to receive intervention on this skill two times a week in our Tier 3 time at the end of the day. We will monitor progress based on IXL.

Source: White River School District, 2018-2019. Used with permission.

Figure 4.2: First-grade SMART goal tracker example.

Use Effective, Research-Based, and Affirmed Instructional Strategies

Collaborative teams are also in control of and have tremendous freedom to discuss and select the researched-based instructional strategies appropriate to advance the work of the standards and learning targets within each unit of study. Teams only know if their instructional strategies are effective with their students when they analyze their data and discuss why their students did well on the formative assessments. That's when the instructional strategies move from being research-based to research-affirmed with students in your school. Once a team has given its first common formative assessment and is looking at the resulting data together, the question naturally arises, "Your kids did better on this than mine did. What did you do?" That is the beginning of the transition from research-based strategies to research-affirmed strategies.

Frequently Monitor and Analyze Evidence of Student Learning

Collaborative teams are also in control of how they use common formative assessment within units of study to support and increase student learning, giving students timely feedback, providing additional time and support for learning, and systematically engaging in the RTI/MTSS process. Having teams develop common formative assessments will do little, if anything, however, to improve student learning if teams do not analyze and use assessment results to affect student learning. Districtwide PLCs ensure that collaborative teams analyze student learning data to make decisions about intervention and extension for students, to improve teacher instructional practices, and enhance team effectiveness (Eaker & Keating, 2012).

Teachers who are new to a district can be anxious about analyzing data. They might have had negative experiences, or they didn't find the task to be productive because there wasn't a protocol to guide conversation and there wasn't an expectation to do anything with the data. At White River, we have found it helpful to think about data analysis in this way: don't just think about the task as analyzing your data. What the team is really doing is coming together to talk about your students and their learning and to celebrate what went well during instruction. As Eaker and Keating (2012) point out:

> At White River, we wanted teams to bring more than student learning data to the table for analysis. We wanted them to also bring student work. This was important because students with the same test scores may have missed different problems or parts of problems. While each team developed its own "personality" or way of doing things, the things teams did as they collaboratively analyzed student learning data were consistent across the district. (p. 124)

The TACA form (see figures 1.2 to 1.6, pages 25–28, in chapter 1) helps teams be more intentional about analyzing student progress toward meeting the unit SMART goals. White River High School teams have made changes to the form to continually improve its efficacy for their teachers and students. First, they added a data box that calculates the number of students proficient or above proficient and those students below proficient on the assessment. These data give teams a way to quickly check progress toward meeting the unit SMART goal. The high school added a specific location for teachers to indicate which students, by name, did not meet the essential standard in the unit SMART goal. The form also includes an area to indicate which teacher is delivering the intervention. (Visit **go.SolutionTree.com** to view a completed sample TACA in Excel spreadsheet form.)

Patsy Gray, instructional facilitator at Hillcrest Elementary in Gillette, Wyoming, shares the following reflection about her work with author Janel Keating to guide the school's PLC work:

> Hillcrest Elementary had collaborative teams that were effectively looking at student data and making informed decisions regarding

interventions and extensions. However, we found that we were still missing an important element in the PLC process—improving adult learning and adult professional practice. We were not having conversations about how we were teaching core Tier 1 instruction. We weren't sharing instructional strategies or talking about engagement or what resources we planned to use during our lessons. There was simply no discussion about daily Tier 1 instruction.

The leadership team decided to add to our protocol. Not only did we decide to analyze some form of student work or data every week but we also added time and a system to explicitly identify the strengths we noticed in student work and list the instructional strategies teacher teams used during Tier 1 instruction. The leadership team updated the protocol, which led to our data reflection protocol [DRP; see figure 4.3]. Here's how it works: every week, each team decides what common student work will be "DRPed" during the next meeting. The protocol guides the conversation and the team's actions. It has made a huge impact on the effectiveness of teams at Hillcrest Elementary and has impacted the results of our Tier 1 instruction. Fewer students need intervention. Weekly teams are building their instructional strategy toolbelt, and it has a powerful impact on Tier 1 instruction. (P. Gray, personal communication, March 11, 2019)

Data Response Protocol (DRP) Week 1
PLC critical questions 3 and 4: How will we respond if some students do not learn it? How will we extend the learning for students who have demonstrated proficiency?
Date: August 29 Assessment Type: Preassessment Weekly Quick Check: Preassessment Scores
Standards or learning targets measured:
Strengths in student work:
Instructional strategies used that helped our students do well:

Trends (Behaviors) in Student Work:			
Far From Proficient	Close to Proficient	Proficient	Advanced

Pretest Results

	Number	Percentage
Advanced		
Proficient		
Close to Proficient		
Far From Proficient		

(Total: 58 students)

Post-Test Results

	Number	Percentage
Advanced		
Proficient		
Close to Proficient		
Far From Proficient		

Things that went well:

Far From Proficient	Close to Proficient	Proficient	Advanced

What do we need to change next year?

What is our plan? Are we going to spend more time in core instruction with these skills or are we going to address them in Tier 2 time? Who is responsible for teaching what skill? How will we assess and decide when to move students from group to group? What is our timeline?

Advanced:

Proficient:

Close to Proficient:

Far From Proficient:

Do we need to tweak or improve this assessment or quick check?

Source: Hillcrest Elementary, 2019. Used with permission.

Figure 4.3: Data response protocol example.

Monitor and Give Feedback on Products and Artifacts

It's our experience at White River that when principals and assistant principals monitor and give feedback to teams on their products and artifacts, they enhance the work of the team. (We listed the artifacts teams produce and use to answer the four critical questions of a PLC at the opening of this chapter.) Teams in White River link their products and artifacts within their unit plan or their monthly team planner. This gives the team and principal or assistant principal direct and immediate access to the products.

On Monday afternoons at White River High School, you'll find Principal Mothershead meeting with assistant principals and the college and career readiness director. The purpose of this meeting is to discuss what each leader observed during collaboration that morning—department by department, team by team. They pull up a chair and project the team unit plans, monthly team planner, or TACA tool. They give feedback starting with simple comments: for example, "I notice . . ." and "I wonder. . . ." The goal of this weekly administrative meeting is to ensure that teacher teams are doing the right work and that expectations are consistent. The administrative team calibrates its thinking by sharing examples and by learning together as well. This meeting is also the time when leaders discuss any issues and brainstorm strategies to help the team function better.

Principal Mothershead shares his thinking regarding the importance of his weekly administrative team meeting to discuss the progress of the teacher teams in the following way:

> Just as teams collaborate, it is critical that the administrative team collaborates when a team is struggling. We will sit down as an administration team and share what we have done or what supports we have put in place. This feedback ensures that our administrative team understands the expectations and directives that have been communicated. This feedback creates consistency so staff members hear the same message from every member of the administrative team. This establishes common expectations and provides clarity for the teacher teams. (C. Mothershead, personal communication, October 7, 2019)

Here's an example of this type of leader monitoring in action: if a team is not consistently using the TACA form to have reflective conversations about student learning, the administrator in charge of that team addresses the issue with the team leader and teacher team. (In White River, our administrative teams split responsibility for the individual teacher collaborative teams.) Also, the administrative team discusses the issue to determine if it is widespread or isolated to a specific team. Administrative team members diagnose reasons for the team not using the TACA and how to respond. Principal Mothershead goes on to say:

> Our administrative team will revisit the progress of the team and its next steps at our next administrative team meeting together. The administrator is usually at the table for the team meeting to see progress; however, if the administrator cannot be at the table, there's follow-up with the team leader right after the meeting to discuss progress toward meeting the expectations. The products and notes from the meeting are transparently available to all, providing a record of the

discussion and the team's next steps. The most effective way to provide guidance to a team is to be at the table and part of the conversation. (C. Mothershead, personal communication, October 7, 2019)

Because this administrative team attends team meetings and reviews team products, members can give specific feedback to teams. Following is an example of specific feedback from Principal Mothershead to the Algebra 2 team:

> Thank you for your intentional work in unit 3A. Your hard work paid off with a near 20 percent growth in the number of students proficient or higher from this same unit last year. Your team's dedication, a detailed unit plan, and the specific interventions you all provided in this unit paid off with over 75 percent of your kids getting to proficient or higher. Thank you for your intentional work with interventions and using student learning data to support the needs of our students. (C. Mothershead, personal communication, May 2, 2019)

We've witnessed school district leaders spending a tremendous amount of time monitoring collaborative meeting minutes rather than team products and artifacts. Just as a team will never improve student learning simply by taking copious notes during its collaborative meetings, a principal or assistant principal will never meet schoolwide improvement goals by reading minutes from collaborative meetings. To improve teacher learning and professional practice, leaders should monitor and give feedback to teams on their products and artifacts.

Provide Additional Time, Support, and Extension for Learning

As Buffum and colleagues (2018) note, "RTI is not an end in itself but a means to an end. It is a tool" (p. 33). We know, based on Hattie's (2009) work, that RTI/MTSS done with fidelity has a high impact on student learning, with an effect size of 1.29. Unfortunately, providing students with intervention and extension is often not done well. Developing an RTI/MTSS process to support student learning has been an evolving journey at White River. Because teachers do a great job of using their collaborative time to focus on all students who need extra time and support, the RTI/MTSS process sometimes feels like an exercise in checking up on teachers, rather than supporting their work and the students they serve.

At White River, we took a step back and refocused on the why: the inverted triangle (figure 4.4, page 102).

We often talk about the importance of teacher teams focusing on the controllable variables; RTI/MTSS is one such controllable variable. In PLCs, the non-negotiables are that every student needs access to and interaction with core curriculum and grade-level standards (Tier 1). We cannot expect to close an education gap for students while also depriving them of access to core learning. Students who struggle with current grade-level standards need access to Tier 2 support. In addition to Tier 1 and Tier 2, some students need Tier 3 supports. A student receiving Tier 3 supports most likely has a significant academic gap, but he or she may also need supports in other areas to become ready to focus on academics.

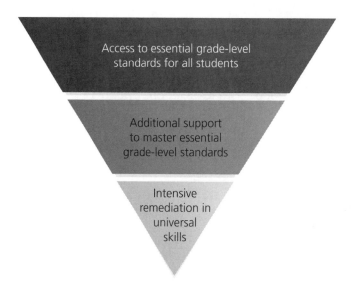

Source: Buffum et al., 2018, p. 22.

Figure 4.4: RTI pyramid showing Tier 1 core instruction and Tier 2 and Tier 3 intervention.

For some students, the school nurse, counselor, or social worker may need to be a part of the whole-child support system that is put in place. At Tier 3, there are often students who need nonacademic supports simultaneously with deeper academic supports. Students experience significant adverse childhood experiences (ACEs) in their lives; the RTI/MTSS meeting is the time and place to address the needs of the whole child.

Each school in White River has an RTI/MTSS coordinator who receives a stipend for the position. This person manages the data used in RTI/MTSS meetings, as well as facilitating the meetings. In addition, the RTI/MTSS coordinator meets monthly for training, to calibrate what is happening in each school and to share ideas.

RTI / MTSS Meetings

This is what RTI/MTSS currently looks like in White River. About every six weeks, each school will spend an entire day in RTI/MTSS meetings. At the elementary level, the grade-level teams each meet for an hour. At the secondary level, content-specific or grade-level teams meet for an hour (for example, the ELA teams might be grade-level teams, but mathematics teams are course specific). We realized that because Tier 3 is not tied close to the core, these meetings don't need to be held around end-of-unit assessments. Three of them are scheduled around benchmarking dates because the benchmark assessment is designed to identify students at high risk. Each school in the district gets floating substitute teachers for the day of its meetings. The principal and RTI/MTSS coordinator design the schedule for the day; floating subs relieve grade-level teams of teachers. A special education teacher and the school counselor are likely there as well. Beyond that, who is present is determined by student needs; for example, the speech therapist, occupational and physical therapist, or the social worker might attend. The goal is that school and district resources wrap around these students.

RTI / MTSS in Action

One of the most difficult issues for schools to address is where to find the time for Tier 3 interventions. How this looks can be different from school to school, and even grade to grade, depending on the number of students receiving interventions and their needs. We know that we cannot close gaps for students without using every resource available. RTI/ MTSS is an integral part of White River's system for getting those resources in place for students who most need them.

In 2015, White River changed its intervention practices. Currently, students with individualized education programs (IEPs) receive core instruction in English language arts and mathematics and then receive their intervention at a separate time. This was a shift in thinking and a change in master schedules. Prior to this, White River had RTI/MTSS meetings, identified student's gaps, and planned Tier 3 interventions. But some students were being pulled from core instruction to go to intervention. As we worked to close the gaps from previous years, these students were simultaneously falling further and further behind in the current year.

Elk Ridge Elementary fourth-grade teacher AnneMarie Allpress remembers this shift in thinking and the difficulty it presented. She notes, "I spent the first two years [of RTI/ MTSS implementation] wiping kids' tears while hearing them say, 'But I don't do your math!' The fourth graders I taught really felt the change and needed to be encouraged often" (A. Allpress, personal communication, June 17, 2019). However, the school began to see the benefits of the RTI/MTSS process with all students receiving core instruction in Tier 1 and then Tier 2 and 3 interventions as needed:

> Last year, I began to notice students relax more in the classroom, knowing that receiving core instruction is an expectation, and that they would be supported through it. This year, I had four students who had IEPs and it was just business as usual for them. They had been doing this system since first grade and knew that they would get support and encouragement as they learned.
>
> Then a pretty cool thing happened: one of the kids with an IEP passed both the English language arts and mathematics Smarter Balanced Assessment this year. Not only did he pass but he also received a score of 4 in English language arts. He is a highly motivated learner who asks questions and strives to know more. He did often say that mathematics was his favorite subject and reading and writing were not. Then he began to gain success this year in our core instruction time for English language arts and started to really take off. All those years of getting double instruction, one at his grade level (Tier 2), and one at his level that was needed to fill the gap (Tier 3) caught up with him.

> When I sat down with the student, his eyes grew huge when he heard his score. He said, "Even in my writing?" and I was able to affirm that he put those skills he'd learned into practice and used spell check and looking back at the text to spell those words that he struggles with. His proud face was my bonus, as well as his K–3 teachers, his instructional paraprofessional, and his special education teacher. I have tried to celebrate with all of them. (A. Allpress, personal communication, June 17, 2019)

Frequently Recognize and Celebrate Accomplishments

White River teams model the importance of celebrating the adults who are working hard with students every day. Some schools avoid celebrating adults for fear that celebrating success will show favoritism or hurt the feelings of staff members who are not being recognized. Here's a way to avoid all those issues and still celebrate.

Start by celebrating the learning of a student or group of students. Share the data with the entire staff. Then call upon the team of teachers and paraeducators who taught these students. Ask these teachers to share what specific strategies they used to help their students learn. When principals use this method to celebrate, everyone learns. Plus leaders are celebrating what the PLC values, which happens to be directly connected to the mission of ensuring learning for all students.

Consider this example from Principal Byrnes:

> When I got my first job as a principal, I wanted to find a way to consistently recognize educators for a job well done. I have always been very passionate about sports, so I thought about ways people are recognized in sports and one example is a game ball. Coaches and players give out a game ball at the conclusion of the game to one person, or a group of people, who went above and beyond. So with that, a tradition was born.
>
> Every time we get together as a staff, someone will give out the game ball—we use a football—to recognize another staff member. Each staff member who receives the game ball signs it and then writes in a notebook why he or she is giving the game ball to the next person. The staff member reads or performs what he or she shared about the next recipient in front of the whole staff. Through the years, I have had people give the awards in a variety of ways, including poems, songs, pictures, raps, or just very heartfelt messages of celebration. (J. Byrnes, personal communication, July 19, 2018)

Figure 4.5 an example of a staff game ball celebration: a game ball given to Janel Ross and Jen Schutz in 2015 by their teammate Noelle Bauer when Noelle was a first-year teacher on a third-grade team. The journal note highlights the sincere appreciation Noelle had for Janel and Jen's mentorship. Fast forward to 2019: Noelle is now a year-four teacher and the team leader. Jen and Janel are now assistant principals in our district.

Dear Janel and Jen,

When I talked with fellow educators about their adventures as a first-year teacher, they said things like, "Prepare to not sleep," "You will have no life," and "This will be the hardest year of your career!" I began to dread my first day in my own classroom. Well, the first day came and went, then months, and now I am standing here today with just three and a half months left of my first year (not that I am counting), and I truly owe it to my teammates. These two individuals laugh with me, cry with me, problem solve with me, listen to me, praise me, encourage me, motivate me, and, most importantly, believe in me. They understand that there is life outside of our jobs, and genuinely put others before themselves on a daily basis. They appreciate the small things in life and understand the importance of a hard laugh. They work hard day and night and treat every student as their own. They love food as much as me and know that you never turn down a cupcake on a student's birthday! They might not remember everything, but they do remember the true meaning of being a teacher. Now, I have no idea where I will be ten years from now, but I do know that with these two women in my life, I will be a better teacher than if I hadn't met them.

Source: Noelle Bauer, 2015. Used with permission.

Figure 4.5: Game ball journal entry from a first-year teacher.

When asked how he celebrates improvements in student learning with his staff, Principal Byrnes shares:

> When we see improvement with a specific grade level, I start by celebrating with the team. We talk about what strategies and interventions they used to help kids learn more. Usually, the team thanks me and then focuses on the three or four students who still need more support! (J. Byrnes, personal communication, July 19, 2018)

Principal Byrnes celebrates with the entire staff by having each team highlight its successes on the last unit or benchmark assessment. Teams then share their next steps and dig into the individual student results. As educational consultant and former superintendent of Adlai Stevenson High School District #125 Timothy Kanold reminded us at our White River administrative retreat in 2019, it's always good for the principal to have a cake budget for staff celebrations (T. Kanold, personal communication, August 2, 2019)!

Celebration doesn't stop with the staff in a districtwide PLC. Ask this question: "Do we recognize and celebrate the things we say we value about our students?" Most schools do a great job of recognizing the students who are on the honor roll or principal's list. There are schools that have elaborate traditions when it comes to recognizing students who excel in the band, choir, and athletic programs. Traditions like earning a school letter for performance or amount of playing time are common. Another typical example of recognition in music and athletics is most valuable player or player of the week awards. While these awards are positive and highlight outstanding performance, they usually do not recognize students who have overcome adversity or made steady improvements over time with their skill and contributions to the group.

What if we really did recognize and celebrate the things that we value about our students? We would continue to recognize students who excel in all academic areas. We would recognize not only perfect attendance but good attendance—five absences or less. It's rare that a staff member has perfect attendance, so why do we hold students to a standard that's beyond a standard we hold for staff? Students experience many home challenges that can impact their attendance, and our students are rarely in control of those. In addition, we have students who suffer with chronic illnesses and will never achieve a perfect attendance award because of that. Teams should also recognize students who have a great attitude and students who put in a tremendous amount of effort. How about students who would never consider breaking a rule? And students who are kind, thoughtful, and respectful every single day? Schools and teams should make time to celebrate the things they say they value about students.

How Collaborative Teams Function

To paint a picture of how grade-level, content-area, and other collaborative teams within White River School District function, we spoke with teacher leaders and teachers within White River schools, who provided in their own words descriptions of their work within collaborative teams. Katie Vail, the fifth-grade team leader at Foothills Elementary, and Fawna Kuntzelman, English department team leader at White River High School, provide the following perspectives into their teams' work and their roles as team leaders. (K. Vail, personal communication, July 25, 2018; F. Kuntzelman, personal communication, December 28, 2019)

The Role of the Team Leader

The role of the team leader is, as Katie notes, being both the rudder and the wind in the sails of the team. The team leader keeps the team on course and sharply focused on the purpose of all students achieving at high levels. It is also the team leader's job to be aware of what teammates need to keep moving toward that goal. The team leader is there to support and hold the team accountable for functioning as a highly effective collaborative team.

The team leader ensures that team members are clear about the focus of Monday morning collaborative meetings. To work effectively, the team needs to be clear about what data and student work members will be looking at and come to the meeting prepared.

As well as providing week-to-week support, the team leader must often think ahead to where the team will need to focus. For example, throughout a unit of study, it's important to think about where the team is in terms of pacing for the year, and where students are in terms of mastering the standards before the unit ends. With teacher-created unit plans, it is crucial for the team leader to ensure that the team stays focused on the essential standards.

A key piece of the team leader role is to be sure that team members are contributing to the work, and to show that member contributions are valued. Collaboration will inevitably have some bumps along the way; teachers don't always have the same thoughts and beliefs about pedagogy. The team leader listens, validates, and asks questions. Team leaders often compromise or agree to explore an instructional strategy and see what the data say. It is reasonable to ask teammates to share research or data to support their views on the strategies they plan to employ with their students. If as a school we are truly committed to student success, the team leader must direct the team in a way that is based on data and research and not personal preference.

Team leaders constantly review grade-level data, student by student, teacher by teacher. Maybe a first-year teammate needs some new strategies to try. Or a third-year teacher who has significantly better data should be teaching a particular intervention for a targeted skill. These are considerations the team leader pursues. The goal is to build a strong team to support students in a thoughtful way that addresses student as well as teacher needs.

Another role of the team leader in White River is to collaborate and communicate with school leadership beyond the leader's grade level. Each school has a building leadership team that discusses data and instructional strategies. The leadership team monitors the school improvement plan and makes decisions for the school based on the needs of every team in the school. As a team leader, these leadership team meetings are a time to advocate for the team and share evidence of what's benefitting students and student achievement. Katie shares the following example:

> My team was successful using paraeducator support in a new way.
> I shared at the team leader meeting that our paraeducators were
> providing extensions for students, and our most struggling learners were
> working with the most qualified classroom teacher. I was able to share
> data that showed this was helping more students achieve at higher
> levels. Several other teams went on to adopt this strategy. (K. Vail,
> personal communication, July 25, 2018)

Kuntzelman shares the following list of roles of the team leader at White River High School. She notes that team leaders attend school-level principal and grade-level and content team meetings and share information with the collaborative team; ensure new teachers have a mentor and understand expectations; plan collaborative time around the four PLC critical questions; and ensure collaborative documents (the TACA form, PLC planner, SMART goals, unit plans, and so on) are updated in a timely manner (F. Kuntzelman, personal communication, December 28, 2019).

Ultimately, team leaders support their team members.

The Collaborative Team Meeting Process

When teams come together for Monday morning collaborative time, they begin by reviewing team norms. Strong team norms are important—they represent what is important to the team and they allow members to hold each other accountable. Then members quickly review the agenda for the meeting. The team leader ensures the agenda is set and that team members receive it the previous week so that everyone comes to the meeting prepared.

The agenda begins with the team looking at data and student work from the previous week. Team members talk honestly, showing trust in one another. When teachers' data differ, team members seek support for best practice—they don't compare and rank teammates based on performance.

After analyzing the data, teams create a plan for the coming week or weeks. Members consider the questions, Do we need to adjust our pacing? Do we need a whole-group reteach? What skill deficits do we need to address during our intervention time? Which students need additional time and support, and who will provide it? Teams do not leave the meeting without a plan that includes what, who, how, and when.

Teams, however, do not limit collaboration to Monday morning meetings. That hour is a tremendous gift; however, team members discuss and strategize during other times as well—common planning times, lunch, in the hallways, and before and after school.

The Unit Plan Skeleton

Every grade level has what's called a unit plan skeleton, created by a cross-district team of teachers and administrators, led by content-area teachers on special assignment, and updated annually. The skeleton contains the essential parts agreed on by the team, including grade-level essential standards by unit, a general pacing guide, key vocabulary, proficiency scales, and any required district preassessments, end-of-unit common assessments, or performance tasks. The plan also contains the standards for the grade below and grade above that are related to each grade-level essential standardand unit progression.

Teams start by breaking the essential standard down into clear learning targets that move the learning from the previous grade level to the next. Teams use their expert knowledge and resources to develop a path for their students to be successful. This learning target pathway is based on student data, so it will be a little different every year. Teams consider the questions, What do students already know coming into the unit? Do they need prerequisite skills built into the learning? Do they already have a strong command of the essential standard?

After the learning target progressions are set, the team begins to plan daily lessons. Each lesson is rooted in learning targets. The daily lessons might be connected to a curriculum that the district provides as a resource or it may take an idea from the curriculum and supplement it with more rigorous work than what the boxed curriculum offered. The daily lessons always represent a collection of the thinking of the team. Peppered in the daily lessons are teacher-created formative assessments.

Each unit plan lays out how the team will reflect on student learning by giving the team members practice showing what they know. From this information, the team makes decisions about instructional moves, pacing, and intervention. Included in the unit plan is the intervention plan. Team members understand that not all students learn at the same rate, so they plan for that. The team records strategies and resources to use with each intervention group in the unit plan, so, if necessary, the team can refer back to this previous work.

Looking at unit plans across a grade level from school to school in the district shows the similar thinking among teams; this is because teams share their work across schools. If a team notices that another school is getting better results on a standard, members open their unit plans to see what they did with their students. They might be looking at instructional strategies, graphic organizers, and performance activities teachers used in lessons, or formative checks, extensions, and interventions. Unit plans continue to evolve every year as teams examine unit plans with fresh eyes and examine what's been learned based on data. No year is exactly the same in terms of unit plans; they have to be different because they are based on data from current students, and student needs differ every year.

Principal Mothershead describes the expectations for collaborative teams and gives detail regarding what that work looks like at the high school.

> We started the process of creating a guaranteed and viable curriculum with team-developed unit plans. In each unit plan, teams list the essential standards followed by sequential learning targets that establish the team's scope and sequence inside the unit. For each target, the team creates success criteria explaining the learning outcomes students need to demonstrate in order to meet that target. The team also links to instructional strategies it has used and found to be effective and a common entry and exit task for each target. Common formative assessments and quick checks for understanding link to each learning target, allowing the team to analyze student learning and create interventions based on that target.

> The unit plan contains critical components including key vocabulary and unit preassessment, which assesses prerequisite skills students should have from previous units or a previous course and end-of-unit common formative assessments. The plan also indicates concepts and skills where students have historically struggled in an effort to help teachers plan additional support in those areas before students struggle again. Within the unit plan, there are links to the TACA form.

> The unit plan and the TACA form also contain the unit SMART goal, which has two parts. The first part of the goal identifies the percentage of students who will be proficient and the skills it takes to be proficient. Teams establish the goals from previous student learning data and knowledge about the students teachers have in their classrooms now. The second part of the goal identifies the essential learning that all students must master at the end of the unit. The team provides specific interventions for students who do not master essential standards.

> In addition to the unit plan, the team creates a proof of progress (POP) sheet students use to self-assess, reflect, and track their progress on each learning target. Teams develop the POP sheets during collaborative team meeting time, aligning them to the agreed-on essential standards

and targets. The team calibrates their scoring of assessments before giving feedback on student work.

Each week, the team decides which exit task or common assessment they will bring to the collaborative team meeting. By having detailed unit plans, teams can use their weekly collaboration time analyzing student work and designing specific and targeted interventions. The team establishes which teacher will be facilitating each intervention group. Students are then assigned to a teacher and a day when they will get the support they need.

The team uses a PLC planning document to ensure there is clarity regarding the agenda for their collaborative team time. The planner includes the items each teacher needs to bring to the table to be prepared. The planner provides clarity for all teams.

There are schoolwide expectations set for collaboration time.

- Data and student work are brought to the table based on formative assessment (TACA): what did you teach last week?

- Use data to design closed intervention sessions. What evidence do we have of student learning (student work)? The data also highlight areas where the instructional strategies were effective and where the teacher or team might need to revisit or reteach a target with the whole class. The team may find it has an instructional issue, not an intervention issue!

- Identify students for each closed intervention session. Who is teaching which skill?

- Bring a positive mindset.

By doing this work, teams at White River High School gain clarity on the four critical questions of a PLC. (C. Mothershead, personal communication, December 30, 2019)

Catherine Uhler, mathematics team leader at White River High School, shares her perspective on how the PLC process has improved learning for students and teachers in the math department:

Our team has evolved from "What are we going to do this week?" (glorified lesson planning) to "What are we going to do for our students this week who are lacking a specific skill?" Bringing student data and work to the table each week is non-negotiable. This work is critical for designing timely interventions around a specific skill. Because of this intentional change of direction and systematic support by our administration, we are closing the skill gap for our kids. Our team has built systems to identify students who need Tier 2 interventions and to hold them accountable to attend Hornet Time interventions. The ability to work with a small group of students, all holding their own whiteboards, is critical to address in-the-moment points of confusion. Building collective efficacy—doing the work of a PLC—on our team has helped us address the needs of all students, not just those on our class roster. It brings me relief each week knowing that I am sending my learners struggling with a specific skill to another teacher for specifically designed interventions, while I work with another group of students on another skill. If we truly are to teach kid by kid, skill by skill, we must intentionally plan, divide, and conquer. The intentional planning and efforts of our team have led to more teachers giving our students more targeted skill interventions during our intervention sessions. That's huge!

We've updated all of our unit plans with SMART goals that reflect essential skills. At the end of each unit, students who have not met the essential skills are listed individually in our TACA form to allow the team to reflect on what we will do collectively to help our learners still struggling with essential concepts and skills in the unit. Even though the unit has passed, the skills are essential for moving forward. We seek out these students with a message of "This is too important to let you slip through the cracks." (C. Uhler, personal communication, December 30, 2019)

Figures 4.6 through 4.9, pages 111–118, show the work of this high school mathematics team.

Geometry Unit 2: Right Triangles and Trigonometry

G.SRT.6: Define and apply trigonometric ratios for acute angles. (claim 1, 2)

G.SRT.7: Use and explain the relationship between sine and cosine of complementary angles. (claim 1, 2)

G.SRT.8: Use trigonometric ratios and the Pythagorean theorem to solve right triangles. (claim 1, 2)

G.MG.2: Apply concepts of density based on area and volume in real world scenarios. (claim 4; for example, persons per square mile, BTUs per cubic foot); *overarching*

G.MG.3: Apply geometric methods to solve design problems. (claim 4); *overarching*

F-TF.3: Use special triangles to determine geometrically the values of sine, cosine, and tangent.

SMART Goal:

We want 60 percent of students to be proficient or higher on the end-of-unit assessment on applying the Pythagorean theorem, and applying right triangle trigonometry. All students will be able to use the Pythagorean theorem or basic trigonometry to find a missing side and angle.

Textbook Lessons: 8.1, 8.2, 8.5

Time Line: 19 days

Vocabulary:

adjacent	opposite
angle of elevation and depression	Pythagorean theorem
complementary	quadratic
cosine	radical
factor	right triangle
hypotenuse	sine
inverse	tangent
leg	trigonometric ratio
	trigonometry

Figure 4.6: Geometry unit plan.

continued ➡

2019–2020 TACA Form

2018–2019 TACA Form

Student Talk:

- How do you know when an answer is in simplest radical form?

- Why do similar triangles have equivalent trigonometry ratios?

- How can we use what we learned about transversals to help us with situations involving angles of elevation and depression?

Preassessment:

Interim Assessment Block Trigonometry Test

Sequential Learning Targets:

1. I can use and apply the Pythagorean theorem. (G.SRT.8; 8.1: p. 344; two days)

   a. This means I (can):

      i. Find the length of a missing side

      ii. Solve quadratic equations that arise in Pythagorean theorem problems (using square roots)

      iii. Write answers in simplest radical form

      iv. Apply the Pythagorean theorem in 2-D applications worksheet 1 or performance task

Assignments: Pythagorean theorem worksheet, word problem worksheet

- Envision 8-1 is the applicable section but the problem sets are largely through the frame of special right triangles.

Entry Task: Warm-up will consist of problems like $x^2 + 25 = 125$ or Pythagorean theorem Edpuzzle (https://bit.ly/3k6lyt0).

Exit Task: (first day) Pythagorean theorem exit

Pythagorean Theorem Quiz

2. I can define and apply trigonometry ratios. (G.SRT.6; Envisions 8.2; six days)

   a. This means I (can):

      i. Know the ratios for sine, cosine, and tangent

      ii. Determine the appropriate trigonometry ratio to solve a problem

      iii. Use trigonometry ratios to find side lengths

      iv. Use inverse trigonometry ratios to find missing angle measures

      v. Apply the trigonometry ratios to real-world applications with right triangles

      vi. Explain and use the relationship between the sine and cosine of complementary angles

- Relay—Right triangles

- MATHO—Right triangles

- History of trigonometry task

- *Mathematics in Three Acts: The Impossible Question* student workbook, p. 203

- Online Envision: 8-2: MathXL for School: additional practice

- Envision 8-2: additional practice worksheet

Entry task: Use on day 2 or 3 or 4.

Exit task or quiz: Quiz (1)—Give quiz after learning target 3. We can then use the data to schedule next steps.

3. I can use trigonometry ratios and Pythagorean theorem involving angles of elevation and depression. (G.SRT.8; two days)

This means I (can):

  i. Correctly identify the angle of elevation and depression

  ii. Apply the Pythagorean theorem

  iii. Apply trigonometry ratios to solve for missing side lengths or angle measures

- Angles of elevation and depression problems (may choose to run as a relay)

- Envision 8-5 number 15–18 (p. 378)

- Envision extra practice and online resources including area problems that we do not want but do have some additional angle of elevation and depression problems

Entry task: Students will work on step 1 of 8-5.

Exit task: one problem; angle of depression

4. I can determine if two triangles are similar by using side ratios and find missing measures. (G.SRT.2; one day)

This means I (can):

  i. Identify similar triangles

  ii. Set up a proportion and solve for a missing side length

  iii. Find angle measures of similar triangles

  iv. Understand the trigonometry ratios are congruent in similar triangles

- Worksheet practice

- Envision 7-5 is the most applicable section but does not really have relevant problem sets.

Entry task: Students will work on 8.2, step 1 (critique and explain activity on p. 191 of their student companion or 8.2: step 1 online)

Exit task: Not needed for prerequisite skill

5. Review (one day) work on more problems like number 2 on the test.

Jeopardy

Assessment (one day)

Assessment:

Test version A

Test version B

Retest

Intervention:

- Simplifying radicals

- Solving square root equations

- Using vocabulary

- Visually representing triangle application problems

- Rounding

- Using notation

- Knowing the difference between finding an angle or finding a ratio (side length)

- Doing multistep problems

continued ➡

For Future:

I can use and apply special right triangles. (F.TF.3; 5-8; three days)

    a. This means I (can):

        i. Know the relationships of side lengths in 45-45-90 and 30-60-90 triangles

        ii. Write answers in simplest radical form

        iii. Find missing side lengths in special right triangles

        iv. Apply to real-world situations

Common Core Tasks:

Trigonometry performance task (sine, cosine, tangent)

Proof of Pythagorean theorem

History of trigonometry

Trigonometry similarity indirect measurement

Baseball trigonometry

Circles and squares (ratios)

Source for standards: NGA & CCSSO, 2010b.

Source: White River School District, 2019. Used with permission.

Proof of Progress Form

Geometry Unit 2: Trigonometry

Common Core State Standards

G.SRT.6: Define and apply trigonmetric ratios for acute angles.

G.SRT.7: Use and explain the relationship between sine and cosine of complementary angles.

G.SRT.8: Use trigonometric ratios and the Pythagorean theorem to solve right triangles.

G.MG.2: Apply concepts of density based on area and volume in real-world scenarios (for example, persons per square mile, BTUs per cubic foot).

G.MG.3: Apply geometric methods to solve design problems.

F-TF.3: Use special triangles to determine geometrically the values of sine, cosine, and tangent.

Learning Targets

    1. I can use and apply the Pythagorean theorem.

    2. I can determine if two triangles are similar by using side ratios and find missing measures.

    3. I can define and apply trigonometry ratios.

    4. I can use trigonometry ratios and the Pythagorean theorem involving angles of elevation and depression.

Daily Work

Date	Learning Target	Assignment	Self-Evaluation
	1	Simplifying square roots worksheet	
	1	Pythagorean theorem word problem worksheet	

	2	Similar triangles worksheet	
	1, 2	Quiz 1	
	3	Worksheet: right triangle trigonometry	
	3	Relay right triangles	
	4	Angles of elevation and depression problems	
	2-4	Trigonometry performance task	
	1-4	Unit 1 test	

Self-Evaluation 4—Totes Got It!; 3—Feeling Good; 2—Getting There; 1—So Lost; 0—What Assignment?!			
Preassessment	**Score / Date**	**Quizzes**	**Score / Date**
Unit 2 preskills		Quiz 1: targets 1 and 2	
Unit 2 test		Quiz 2: targets 3 and 4	
Learning Target	**Learning Target**		
1	I can use and apply the Pythagorean theorem. I can find the length of a missing side. ☐ I can solve quadratic equations. ☐ I can write answers in simplest radical form. ☐ I can apply the Pythagorean theorem in 2-D and 3-D applications.		
2	I can determine if two triangles are similar by using side ratios and find missing measures. I can identify similar triangles. ☐ I can set up a proportion and solve for a missing side length. ☐ I can find angle measures of similar triangles.		
3	I can define and apply trigonometry ratios. I know the ratios for sine, cosine, and tangent. ☐ I understand that trigonometry ratios are congruent in similar triangles. ☐ I can determine the appropriate trigonometry ratio to solve a problem. ☐ I can use trigonometry ratios to find side lengths of right triangles. ☐ I can use inverse trigonometry ratios to find missing angle measures in right triangles. ☐ I can apply the trigonometry ratios to real-world applications with right triangles. ☐ I can explain and use the relationship between the sine and cosine of complementary angles.		
4	I can use trigonometry ratios and the Pythagorean theorem involving angles of elevation and depression. ☐ I can correctly identify the angle of elevation and depression. ☐ I can apply the Pythagorean theorem. ☐ I can apply trigonometry ratios to solve for missing side lengths or angle measures.		

Source for standards: NGA & CCSSO, 2010b.

Source: White River School District, 2019. Used with permission.

Figure 4.7: Geometry proof of progress.

White River High School Geometry   Name: _____

For each triangle shown below, find the missing side. Box your answer.

Basic

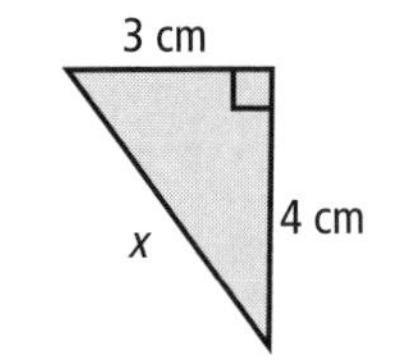

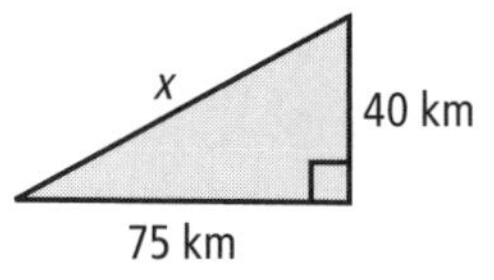

Proficient

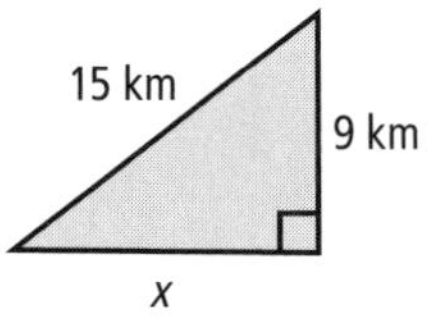

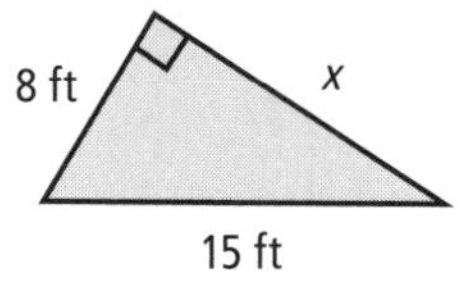

Mastery

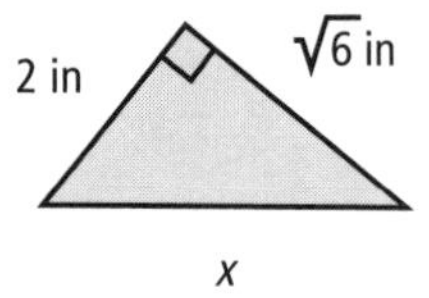

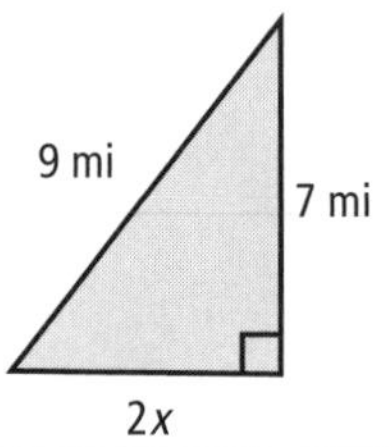

Source: White River School District, 2019. Used with permission.

Figure 4.8: Geometry common formative check for understanding.

Name: _____   Date: _____   Period: _____

Unit 2: Right Triangle Test A

Show all work and label all answers to receive full credit.

Basic

1. Which of the following would be used to find an unknown side? **(Circle all that apply.)**

        a. $\cos 61°$ b. $\tan^{-1} 2.9$ c. $\sin 41°$ d. $\tan D°$ e. $\cos^{-1} 0.72$

2. Triangle *ABC* is similar to triangle *WYZ*.

Select two angles whose tangent equals $\frac{3}{4}$.

    a. $\angle A$

    b. $\angle B$

    c. $\angle C$

    d. $\angle W$

    e. $\angle Y$

    f. $\angle Z$

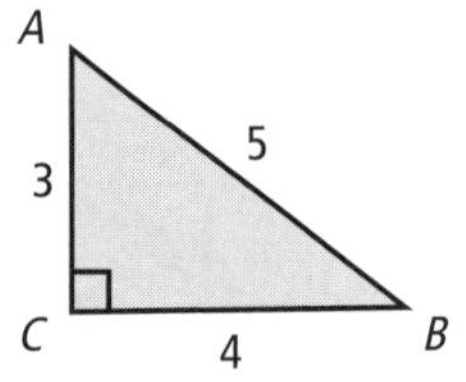

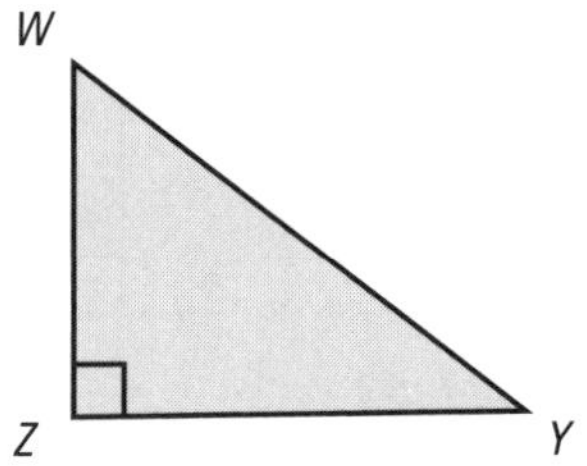

3. A pilot flying at an altitude of 2.8 km sights the runway directly in front of her. The distance from the airplane to the runway is 5.6 km. What is the horizontal (ground) distance, *TR*, to the runway? Round to the nearest tenth of a kilometer.

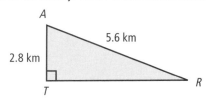

Proficient

4. Find all unknown measures.

4*GH* = _____

GF = _____

m ∠ G = _____

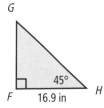

5. Find all unknown measures.

AB = _____

m ∠ A = _____

m ∠ B = _____

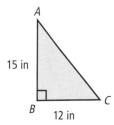

6. Jessie is building a ramp for loading motorcycles onto a trailer. The trailer is 2.9 feet off the ground. To avoid making it too difficult to push a motorcycle up the ramp, Jessie decides to make the angle between the ramp and the ground 15°. Sketch this situation and find the length of the ramp.

7. In $\triangle ABC$, $\angle B$ is a right angle. If Cos $A = \frac{2}{3}$, what is Sin *C*? Draw $\triangle ABC$ to support answer.

Mastery

8. Marcus is flying a plane at an altitude of 1,700 ft. He sights a monument at an angle of depression of 32°.

    a. What is Marcus's approximate horizontal distance from the monument?

    b. What is Marcus's approximate real distance from the monument?

Figure 4.9: Geometry common end-of-unit assessment.   continued ➡

9. Find the following using the figure to the right:

$m \angle DAB =$ _____

$m \angle DBC =$ _____

$y =$ _____

$x =$ _____

10. Triangle *ABC* is similar to triangle *WYZ*.

Determine whether each statement is true. Select *true* or *false* for each statement.

	True	False
$\sin(A) < \sin(Y)$		
$\cos(B) = \sin(W)$		
$\tan(W) > \tan(A)$		

Source: White River School District, 2019. Used with permission.

Tools for Team Planning

Collaborative teams in the White River School District use tools for team planning that increase transparency and allow for team members to collaborate both during and outside of meeting time. These include a platform to facilitate transparent collaboration, a monthly planning tool, and district-developed resources for unit planning.

A Platform for Transparent Collaboration

White River School District has a Google site; using Google districtwide allows White River to create a platform where collaboration and transparency become very easy, not only face to face but digitally. It required a shift in thinking for collaborative teams and staff to make the move to using shared online documents and folders, but people quickly realized what a benefit it was. Cloud computing with Google allows our teachers to work collaboratively on a document from remote locations, view the work that other teams are doing, and share their work with their administrative team without having to email things back and forth and without getting lost in that forest of files trying to determine which version is the most recent.

Collaborative teams use what White River calls *The Work sites*. These sites provide a location for shared working files so that administrative teams can always locate current documents when accessing a TACA form or updated unit plan. They are called *The Work sites* because they contain every piece of the important work teams do every day. The sites house continuous improvement cycles, scope and sequence documents, unit plans, TACA forms, assessments, and all the resources a team develops; they house the guaranteed and viable curriculum in White River. The sites make it possible to archive and save previous iterations of documents, but current work is always easy to find. The Work sites are accessible to all teaching staff—a fourth-grade teacher at one elementary school can easily open the unit 2 plans from a fourth-grade team at another elementary school and see what resources they have developed. A ninth-grade English language arts teacher at the high school can look at the eighth-grade unit plans at the middle school to see what essential standards teams focus on and how they were taught. Paraprofessional support teams can look ahead and preteach something from an upcoming unit or lesson.

There are three Work sites for White River schools—one site for elementary, one for middle, and one for high school (see figures 4.10–4.15, pages 119–122).

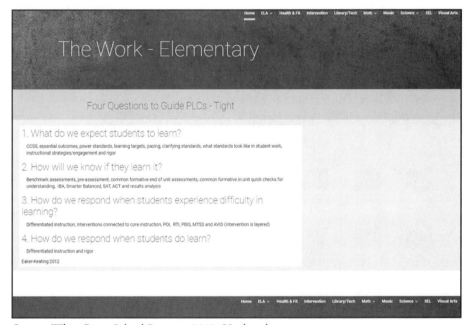

Source: White River School District, 2019. Used with permission.

Figure 4.10: Elementary The Work site home page.

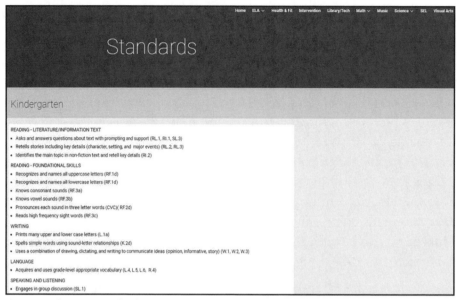

Source: White River School District, 2019. Used with permission.

Figure 4.11: State standards by grade and content area.

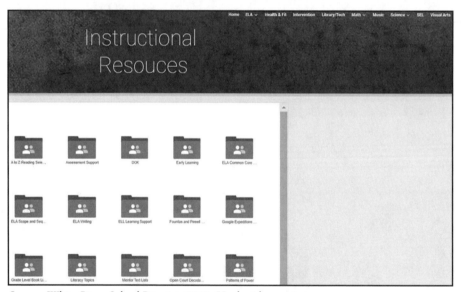

Source: White River School District, 2019. Used with permission.

Figure 4.12: Resources for teachers and teams.

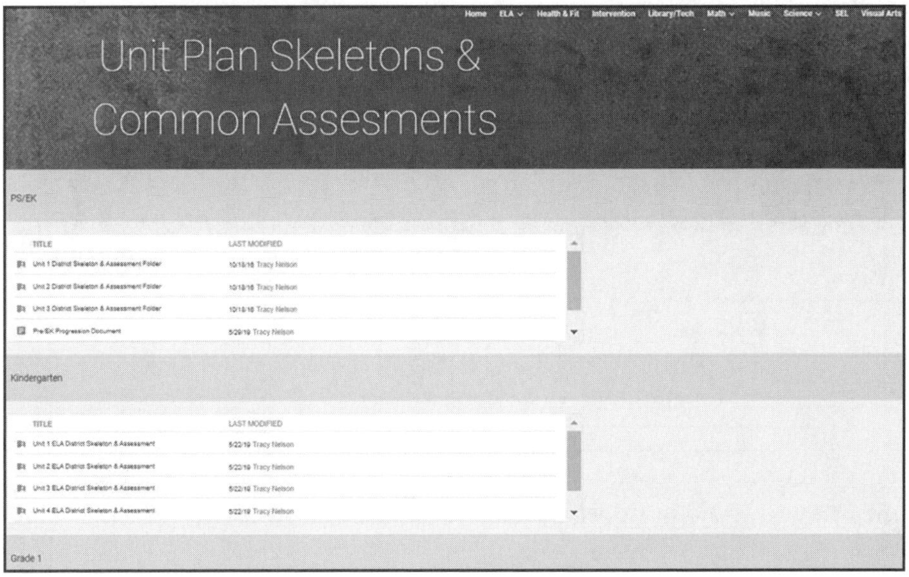

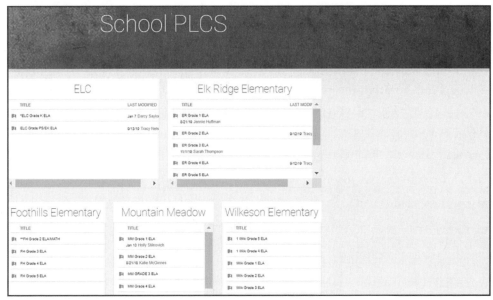

Source: White River School District, 2019. Used with permission.

Figure 4.13: Unit plan skeletons and common assessments.

Source: White River School District, 2019. Used with permission.

Figure 4.14: School PLC folders.

Source: White River School District, 2019. Used with permission.

Figure 4.15: Data that show the overall student achievement levels from each school.

Monthly Planning Tool

At White River, we expect that every collaborative team uses a planning tool. White River doesn't micromanage what that tool looks like; rather, the district wants to ensure that every team comes prepared for collaboration. The monthly planning tool must be accessible to everyone on the staff to view. It's very helpful for special education, English learning educators, and Title I staff to be able to view at a glance what teams are doing to determine which collaboration meeting to attend. It should only take a couple of minutes for the team to complete the necessary elements in the planning tool for each meeting. They consider the following questions.

- When will we hold the meeting?
- What is the plan for the meeting?
- What will we bring?

And after the meeting they add:

- What did we accomplish?
- What are our next steps for collaboration, and what do we agree to bring to the table?
- Do we need help from an administrator or another team, and if so, what help?

Team leaders want to ensure all team members prepare to attend the collaborative team meeting. The monthly planning tool is an effective way for the team leader to remind the team and clarify expectations when texting or emailing prior to collaboration.

White River teams create the PLC monthly planner in a Google Doc. This document highlights the expectations for collaborative time and has a place for team norms as well as an overall yearlong team SMART goal. Keep in mind, teams will also be setting a SMART goal unit by unit. These goals appear in their unit plans. Meeting unit-by-unit

SMART goals is the avenue to meeting the overall yearlong SMART goal. Teams often link their products directly in this planning tool as it's a quick place for the team and administration to access the work. The planning tool is designed to be viewed by the entire elementary school or an entire department at the secondary level. For example, team 1 could be kindergarten, team 2 could be first grade, team 3 could be second grade, and so on. At the high school, the planning tool would be by department; team 1 would be grade 9 English, team 2 grade 10 English, team 3 grade 11 English, and so on.

District-Developed Resources for Unit Planning

As Eaker and Keating (2015) explain:

> Collaborative teams in a PLC emphasize how they think about planning a unit of instruction. They are much more concerned about focusing on the right questions than they are about the correct format. In one sense, collaborative unit planning is a perfect example of the simultaneous loose-tight framework in action. The team collaboratively agrees on a number of things that it will be tight about regarding each unit, but be loose regarding teacher methodology or instructional approaches. Teachers in a PLC are constantly reminded that teacher autonomy and creativity are not only allowed but, in fact, encouraged—within the set parameters of collaboratively developed units of instruction. While there is no one right way to teach, teacher teams engage in deep discussion about instructional effectiveness, reflecting on notes that were kept from previous years regarding what seemed to work and what didn't work so well, and then share these instructional ideas and materials. (p. 55)

Let's take a look at an example of the rationale behind the creation of a unit plan: the purpose of the White River School District English language arts unit plans, common assessments, and pacing guide is to design a clear and coherent instructional and professional development district plan for ELA instruction in grades 3, 4, and 5 for the school year. In other words, what do we want our students to know and be able to do? Essentially, the plan allows teachers to deliver a guaranteed and viable curriculum across the district.

At the district level, a guiding coalition identified the three priority standards (key ideas) in reading and writing. In reading, these include both literary and information standards. In writing, these include opinion pieces, information and explanatory texts, and narratives. The ELA units of study one through three will be based on the Imagine It themes, target one reading and writing standard per unit, and then repeat for units four through six. A minimal unit template has been initiated for grades 3, 4, and 5. Site-based grade-level teams are empowered to further develop these unit plans based on student needs and instructional resources. To ensure that students learn the reading foundations standards, teachers are expected to teach the explicit phonemic, phonic, and fluency concepts for each lesson.

Each unit will have grade-level-created common pre- and postassessments. The purpose of these assessments is to inform grade-level teams of their students' knowledge and skills and determine the next instructional steps. At the district level, these assessments will help inform our district practice, resource allocation, and professional development plan. In other words, how will we know students are learning? Several units will have grade-level-created performance tasks. The purpose of those performance tasks is to challenge students to apply their knowledge and skills to respond to complex real-world problems. They can best be described as collections of questions and activities that are coherently connected to a single theme or scenario. These activities are meant to measure capacities such as depth of understanding, writing and research skills, and complex analysis, which cannot be adequately assessed with traditional assessment questions.

Some school districts—White River included—provide teams with unit planning tools that include some of the elements collaborative teams work to develop together. These consist of such materials as a unit planning skeleton for specific subjects that include essential standards and end-of-unit common formative assessments; district-adopted curriculum resources, such as unit plans, pacing guides, common formative assessments, scoring guides, and TACA forms; and the traditional curriculum resources that districts supply. Collaborative grade-level and content-area teams might wonder how these materials fit into the collaborative team process when answering the four critical questions of a PLC. How do teams enhance already existing resources?

Molly Curran, the grade 4 team leader at Mountain Meadow Elementary, provides insight in this section into how her team uses district-developed resources strategically to constantly improve and support the ongoing endeavor of more students learning at higher levels every day.

It is important to note that White River worked to establish a guaranteed and viable curriculum and put systems and resources in place to support the work of collaborative teams—not to micromanage and dictate every instructional move:

> After working in a district where I had some experience building unit plans from scratch, being given an existing unit plan skeleton with preidentified standards, essential questions, learning targets, and meaningful resources offered a sense of relief. A great deal of work had clearly already been done, but that presented a different type of challenge. Since I was not present in the creation of this work, the existing skeleton did not necessarily meet my team's specific needs; and, more importantly, it didn't always meet the specific needs of our students that year. What we lacked was ownership in these unit plans.

> Let's be clear, I was incredibly thankful to be inheriting unit plans because it was my first time ever teaching fourth grade. I understood it was a skeleton, and a place to start. Initially, I was apprehensive about some of the content and I wanted to make sure that I fully understood the curriculum, the resources, and the grade-level standards. Before the start of the school year, I began looking through the existing unit plans and realized portions of the unit plans lacked consistency. For example, the essential questions in one unit were written as specific questions to ask the students to check for understanding. Yet in the following unit, the identified essential questions were reflective ideas that the teacher should consider throughout the unit to check for student understanding.

Further, I realized that the grade-level standards taught in the units lacked clarity and required the teachers to look elsewhere to gain a better understanding.

As educators, we know the teachers who originally created the unit planning document most likely totally understood exactly why they made the choices the tool reflected. Like any tool, however, it is only valuable to users if they also fully understand all of its attributes. Therefore, a cross-district team of fourth-grade teachers worked together to better understand the existing unit plans, make them more consistent, and better align the unit plans to the grade-level standards. The district gave us a place to start; we were given the freedom to put meat on the bone of that plan.

When the team of teachers sat down to begin this work, we quickly discovered determining exactly which lessons in the district-adopted curriculum aligned to specific grade-level standards presented a daunting challenge. The identified list of standards for each lesson was often lengthy, when in reality a specific lesson only addressed one or two clear targets, skills, or concepts adequately. Discovering how difficult this work would be was concerning; however, the team could not teach these skills and concepts effectively without fully understanding how they were designed to be addressed in each individual lesson. Even further, without understanding how well the curriculum connected to these standards, we knew that we could not make wise instructional moves when determining what essentials must be taught exactly as written and what lessons should be taught in a different way to give students better access to content. This struggle is true with many adopted resources.

Next, as a team, we created a structure through our unit plans, as well as individual lessons, that allowed us to look critically at each lesson to discern when and how each standard is taught. Doing this work helped us determine essential standards unit by unit, and the logical next step was to align those grade-level concepts with the grade levels above and below. This effort enabled me to think beyond fourth grade as I could reference prior learning, as well as offer students better access to the skills and concepts that are still to come in the next grade level.

After gaining a deeper understanding of the essential standards in each unit, it became apparent that our end-of-unit assessments did not adequately focus on the required learning associated with that unit. For example, an assessment with twenty questions might only have five questions directly related to the essential learning of that period of instruction. Needless to say, when reflecting on student results, the fact that students could correctly answer the majority of items, but possibly still lack mastery of the most important standards of the unit, presented a significant problem that the team needed to address. The most experienced fourth-grade teachers were still able to use the data collected from the existing assessments well; however, systemically, it was difficult for teachers to effectively use these assessment results to support their students.

Due to the work that our team had done to understand the various units, we could immediately address this problem by working to create more targeted formative assessments, which provided constant feedback on the needs of the class related to the most crucial skills and concepts unit by unit. Although this helped us better support our student needs, it didn't yet offer a solution to the fact that our assessments lacked both rigor and focus. Now with a new challenge to face, the work shifted toward a district-level push to rewrite assessments that focused on students demonstrating understanding, rather than accumulating points. This opportunity allowed us to become involved in creating a proficiency scale assessment structure for not only my teacher team but the entire district.

Again, with a team of teachers, the work began with analyzing current assessments in order to make strategic choices to improve instruction moving forward. This process, which continues even today, requires constant discussion, updates, edits, and revisions to ensure that year after year these assessments are seen as tools with which teachers gain insight into student knowledge, rather than simply as must-do tasks on a long list of the requirements of the modern educator. I am proud to share that after the district-level fourth-grade team piloted these tests, they reached the greatest levels of mathematics achievement on the state standardized tests in our district's history with the Smarter Balanced Assessment. (M. Curran, personal communication, September 20, 2019)

It is important for a team to do this work to become better educators and to record the process in such a way that any teacher can access, use, and develop it further. Molly Curran and the teachers who redesigned the fourth-grade unit plans laid the groundwork for improved mathematics instruction for years to come. While the documents continue to be updated and improved year after year, it was the work of that initial team to create a structure that other teams continue to benefit from. Grade-level teams from kindergarten through fifth grade now use the unit plan structure that Molly's fourth-grade team created for its own clarity on essential standards within the unit as well as additional learning that takes place.

Figure 4.16 and figure 4.17, page 132, are additional examples of a unit plan and a pacing guide for mathematics.

Singletons and Collaborative Work

Many district leaders and teachers wonder how singleton teachers work collaboratively in teams within a PLC. How do singletons collaborate to impact professional practice when they are the only ones who teach their content? Do singletons need to create a unit plan

Grade Level: 4	Time Period: March 11 to April 19	Content Area: Mathematics

Unit 6: Multiplication, Division, Data, and Fractions		

Essential Learning to Be Mastered	Additional Learning	SMART Goals

Essential Learning to Be Mastered

- Multiply a one- or two-digit whole number by a one- or two-digit whole number, or two two-digit numbers using strategies based on place value and the properties of operations. Use equations and rectangular arrays to explain strategies for multiplying with multidigit numbers.

- Divide a two-, three-, or four-digit number by a one-digit number, with or without a remainder, using strategies based on place value, the properties of operations, or the relationship between multiplication and division. Use equations and rectangular arrays to explain strategies for dividing a multidigit number by a one-digit number.

- Apply the area or perimeter formulas for a rectangle to solve a problem.

- Make a line plot to display a data set of measurements in fractions of a unit ($\frac{1}{2}$, $\frac{1}{4}$, $\frac{1}{8}$). Solve problems involving addition and subtraction of fractions by using information presented in line plots.

- Demonstrate an understanding that a fraction $\frac{a}{b}$ is a multiple of the unit fraction $\frac{1}{b}$; write an equation showing that a fraction $\frac{a}{b}$ is the product of a x $\frac{1}{b}$ (number corner check up).

- Multiply a fraction by a whole number; demonstrate an understanding that any multiple of $\frac{a}{b}$ is also a multiple of the unit fraction $\frac{1}{b}$ (NCCU).

- Solve story problems that involve multiplying a fraction by a whole number (NCCU).

- Express a fraction with denominator 10 as an equivalent fraction with denominator 100 (NCCU).

- Add a fraction with denominator 10 to a fraction with denominator 100 by rewriting the first fraction as an equivalent fraction with denominator 100 (NCCU).

- Compare two decimal numbers with digits to the hundredths place (NCCU).

- Identify an angle as a geometric figure formed where two rays share a common endpoint (NCCU).

- Demonstrate understanding that an angle is measured with reference to a circle with its center at the common endpoint of the rays, by considering the fraction of the circular arc between the points where the two rays intersect the circle. An angle that turns through $\frac{1}{360}$ of a circle is called a "one-degree angle" and can be used to measure angles (NCCU).

- Identify the measure of an angle by identifying the total number of one-degree angles through which it turns (NCCU).

Additional Learning

- Solve multistep story problems involving whole numbers, using all four operations, including division with remainders.

- Find all factor pairs for a whole number between 1 and 100; demonstrate an understanding that a whole number is a multiple of each of its factors.

- Generate a number of shape patterns that follow a given rule. Identify apparent features of the pattern that were not explicit in the rule itself.

- Use the standard algorithm with fluency to add and subtract multidigit whole numbers

- Recognize and generate equivalent fractions.

- Compare two fractions with different numerators and different denominators.

- Understand that addition and subtraction of fractions as joining and separating parts referring to the same whole.

- Decompose a fraction into a sum of fractions with the same denominator in more than one way, recording each decomposition by an equation.

- Add mixed numbers and fractions with a like denominator.

- Use a protractor to measure angles in whole degrees; sketch an angle of a specified measure.

- Decompose an angle into non-overlapping parts; express the measure of an angle as the sum of the angle measure of the non-overlapping parts into which it has been decomposed.

- Draw points, lines, line segments, rays, angles (right, acute, obtuse), and perpendicular and parallel lines. Identify these in 2-D figures.

- Classify 2-D figures based on the presence or absence of parallel or perpendicular lines or the presence or absence of angles of a specified size; identify right triangles.

SMART Goals

By the end of unit 6, 85 percent of our students will be able to divide four-digit numbers by a one-digit number as measured by question 5 on the end of unit assessment and CFA. The remaining 15 percent of students will be able to divide two-digit numbers by a one-digit number as measured by a teacher-created common formative assessment.

Figure 4.16: Grade 4 mathematics unit plan.

continued ➡

Standards Addressed in This Unit

Major Clusters	Supporting Clusters	Additional Clusters
4.OA.A: Use the four operations with whole numbers to solve problems.	**4.OA.B:** Gain familiarity with factors and multiples.	**4.OA.C:** Generate and analyze patterns.
4.NBT.B: Use place value understanding and properties of operations to perform multidigit arithmetic.	**4.MD.A:** Solve problems involving measurement and conversion of measurements.	**4.MD.C:** Geometric measurement: understand concepts of angle and measure angles.
4.NF.A: Extend understanding of fraction equivalence and ordering.	**4.MD.B:** Represent and interpret data.	**4.G.A:** Draw and identify lines and angles and classify shapes by properties of their lines and angles.
4.NF.B: Build fractions from unit fractions.		
4.NF.C: Understand decimal notation for fractions and compare decimal fractions.		

Sandwiched Learning Progressions

Continuum of Learning: Operations and Algebraic Thinking, Numbers and Base 10, Fractions

Grade Below	Grade Level	Grade Above
*No line plots taught	**4.NBT.5:** Multiply a whole number of up to four digits by a one-digit whole number, and multiply two two-digit numbers, using strategies based on place value and the properties of operations. Illustrate and explain the calculation by using equations, rectangular arrays, and/or area models.	**5.MD.B.2:** Use operations on fractions for this grade to solve problems involving information presented in line plots.
3.NBT.A2-3: Fluently add and subtract within 1,000. Multiply one-digit whole numbers by multiples of 10.		**5.NBT.B.5-6:** Find quotients of whole numbers with up to four-digit dividends and two-digit divisors. Add, subtract, multiply, and divide decimals to hundredths.
3.OA.D.8: Solve two-step word problems using the four operations.	**4.NBT.6:** Find whole-number quotients and remainders with up to four-digit dividends and one-digit divisors, using strategies based on place value, the properties of operations, and/or the relationship between multiplication and division. Illustrate and explain the calculation by using equations, rectangular arrays, and/or area models.	
3.MD.C.5-7: Find area using tiles, counting squares, and multiplying side lengths.		**5.OA.A.1:** Use parentheses, brackets, or braces in numerical expressions, and evaluate.
3.MD.D.8: Solve real-word problems involving perimeter of polygons.	**4.MD.3:** Apply the area and perimeter formulas for rectangles in real-world and mathematical problems. *For example, find the width of a rectangular room given the area of the flooring and the length by viewing the area formula as a multiplication equation with an unknown factor.*	**5.MD.C:** Recognize volume as an attribute of solid figures and understand concepts of volume measurement.
	4.MD.4: Make a line plot to display a data set of measurements in fractions of a unit (, ,). Solve problems involving addition and subtraction of fractions by using information presented in line plots. *For example, from a line plot find and interpret the difference in length between the longest and shortest specimens in an insect collection.*	

Key Vocabulary

dividend	remainder	area	quotient	median	dimension
divisor	line plot	perimeter	partial products	mode	data
equivalent ratio	range				

Student-Friendly Learning Targets Learning Target Booklet				Links to Assessments and Evidence
Measurement and Data	**Numbers and Base 10**	**Operations and Algebraic Thinking**	**Fractions**	

	Links to Assessments and Evidence
Module 1: I can choose the most efficient strategy to solve multidigit multiplication and division problems. **Module 2:** I can use area and perimeter to solve real-world problems and find unknown factors. **Module 3:** I can use a line plot to solve problems (addition, subtraction, measurements involving fractions). **Module 4:** I can use division to solve real-world problems.	Unit preassessment Unit postassessment Reflection Scoring guide **Bridges Checkpoints** Area and perimeter **Teacher-Created Formative Assessment** Multiplication and division check 1 Math Club quick check 1 Math Club quick check 2 **IAB Given** Operations and algebraic thinking Operations and algebraic thinking entrance slips

Additional Resources

Workplace Games	**Home Connections**	**Bridges Next Steps**
Unit 6 workplace log	Week 1	Bridges assessment and resource opportunities
6A: Factors and multiples directions	Week 2	
Factors and multiples record sheet	Week 3	Bridges assessment document
6B: Area or perimeter directions	Week 4	
Area or perimeter record sheet	Week 5	Bridges skills across the grade level
6C: Fraction spin and add directions		
Fraction spin and add record sheet		
6D: Lowest remainder wins directions		
Lowest remainder wins record sheet		
Lowest remainder wins challenge record sheet		

continued ➡

Interventions	Extensions	Additional Fluency Games
Math Club quick check 1 Math Club quick check 2 Based on the weekly checks, we put students into the following groups. • Addition • Subtraction • Multiplication • Division • Task cards Multiplication task cards (2 × 2) Multiplication task cards (4 × 1) Multiplication story problems level 1 Multiplication story problems levels 2–3 Division task cards (3 by 1) One-digit divisor task cards Two-digit divisor task cards	Resort report packet (multiplication focus) Cinema packet (division focus) Cinema packet advanced (division focused)	Four in a Row (multiplying by 10 and 100) Race to Finish (multiplying one-digit numbers by multiples of 10, 100, and 1,000) Roll a Row (multiplying double-digit multiples of 10) Snakes (two-digit by two-digit multiplication to 20) Snakes (multiplying three- and four-digit numbers by one-digit numbers) Squares (multiplying two-digit numbers) Squares (multiplying and dividing by 10 and 100) Tic Tac Toe (multiplying two-digit and one-digit numbers)

Day-to-Day Planning

Day 1	Day 2	Day 3	Day 4	Day 5
MM: $72 \div 6 = a$ **CGI:** Sydnee, Hope, Darren, and Brady had a bake sale. They made a total of $148. If the four kids split the money equally, how much money will each kid get? **Extension:** Hope went to the mall to spend some of her money. She bought 2 shirts that cost $8.75 each. How much money does Hope have left?	**MM:** $3 \times a = 42$ **CGI:** The fourth graders at Mountain Meadow are having a pizza party. The teachers paid a total of $126. If each pizza cost $7, how many pizzas did they order? **Extension:** The teachers want to be sure to give each of the 4 classes an equal amount of slices to share with their students. If each pizza has 8 slices, how many slices will each of the 4 classes get?	**MM:** $19 \times 4 = a$ **CGI:** Mrs. Akins went to the 99 Cent Store and bought earbuds for her students. If she bought a total of 26 earbuds for 99 cents each, how much money did she spend? **Extension:** She also decided to buy her class popsicles while she was at the 99 Cent Store. If the popsicles come in packs of 4, how much money will she spend to give each of her 26 students a popsicle?	**MM:** $56 - (3 \times 12)$ **CGI:** Brohdy and his teammates have been selling coupon cards to help raise money for his soccer team. They raised a total of $316. They want to use the money to buy new uniforms for their team. There are a total of 12 boys on the team and each uniform costs $24. How much money will they have left over? **Extension:** With their leftover money, they want to buy new socks. Each pair of socks costs $3.25. How many pairs of socks can they buy with the leftover money?	**MM:** $(12 \times 3) \div 6$ **CGI:** Miss Weber went to the store to buy pencils for her class. She bought 16 packs of pencils. Each pack has 12 pencils. When she got to school, she divided the pencils evenly among the 6 tables in class. How many pencils will each table get? **Extension:** Miss Weber bought the packs of pencils at a 99 Cent Store. How much money did she spend?

Multiplication and Division Formative	**Day 6**	**Day 7**	**Day 8**	**Day 9**
$24 \times 32 = x$ $300 \div 8 = x$ $9 \text{ ft} \times a = 351 \text{ ft}^2$ The Mountain Meadow PTA is buying Valentines for all of the students at the school. They bought 24 boxes of 16 Valentines and 18 boxes of 22 Valentines. There are 512 students at Mountain Meadow. Did they buy enough Valentines to give one to each student? If so, how many do they have left over? If not, how many more do they need?	**MM:** $100 - (5 \times 11) = d$ **CGI:** Avalon has been saving her money for the past several months to go on a shopping spree! She brought $150 to the mall and bought 3 shirts that cost $21 each and 5 books that cost $16 each. How much money does she have left? **Extension:** Before she left the mall, she used her leftover money to buy 3 bracelets that cost $1.75 each. How much money does she have left now?	**MM:** $96 \div 6 = q$ **CGI:** Naomi is helping her mom put wallpaper on the wall. She knows the area of the room is 264 ft² and one dimension is 12 feet. What is the other dimension of the room? **Extension:** Naomi and her mom are going to wallpaper all four of the walls in her room. If the wallpaper comes in rolls that can cover 120 ft², how many rolls of wallpaper will they need to cover all four walls?	**MM:** $24 \times 20 = a$ $24 \times 9 = b$ $24 \times 29 = c$ **CGI:** Dayton's mom ordered 4,000 beads to make necklaces. She used the beads to make 33 necklaces with 29 beads in each. She got a second order for 44 necklaces with 62 beads on each. If she has enough beads, how many will she have left over? If she does not have enough, how many more will she need? **Extension:** How many 29-bead necklaces will she be able to make with her leftover beads?	**MM:** Draw a rectangle: **Perimeter** = 36 cm **One Dimension** = 8 **Find Area** **CGI:** Brodee ran the perimeter of the football field to warm up for lacrosse practice. If the total perimeter is 364 yards and one of the dimensions is 127 yards, what is the length of the other side? **Extension:** What is the area of the football field?

Day 10

MM: $98 \times 5 = a$

$98 \times 5 = (100 \times 5) - (\underline{\hspace{2cm}} \times \underline{\hspace{2cm}})$

Cognitively guided instruction: Bryce was solving the problem $98 \times 47 = p$. He decided to use the over strategy. He wrote the equation $(100 \times 47) - (2 \times 98) = p$.

Your job is to solve $98 \times 47 = p$ and explain whether or not Bryce will get to the correct answer using his equation.

Extension: Max was solving the problem $86 \times 78 = p$. He decided to use the distributive property to save space on his paper. He wrote the equation $(80 \times 70) + (6 \times 8) = p$.

Your job is to solve $86 \times 78 = p$ and explain whether or not Max will get to the correct answer using his equation.

continued ➡

2018–2019 Reflection Notes

Celebrations: We were very pleased with how well the students did finding a dimension of a path when the area and one dimension were given. Students demonstrated a really strong number sense to efficiently divide 7,049 by 7. We noticed students' attention to detail in providing the correct label in their answers, especially number 7 when being asked to provide the number of minutes in a school (not hours and minutes). Students are using efficient strategies to multiply and divide. We also noticed more students did well with the property work of number 1.

Instructional strategies: We reviewed area and perimeter during number corner. We have been really intentional with our number choices to help build efficiency, number sense, and property work. We provide students with daily problem solving that involves multistep problems, area, and perimeter. During this unit, we gave weekly formatives to adjust math groups as needed—each group focusing on a different operation of whole numbers. Daily entrance slips also provided students quick review of property work as well.

Misconceptions: Students need to develop an understanding of reasonableness in working with area and perimeter of a rectangles (if the perimeter is 734 cm, is it reasonable that one dimension is 3,000 cm?). Students need to start thinking about how they can explain what they are thinking rather than just acting. We need to continue our work with place value—many students are still developing this skill but need additional practice with the skill.

Source for standards: NGA & CCSSO, 2010b.

Source: White River School District, 2019. Used with permission.

White River School District Mathematics Pacing Guide, 2019–2020, Grade 4

Units 1–3 for first semester, Units 4–7 for second semester *to be updated 08/30/19 as a grade-level team*

Unit	Name	Clusters Assessed	Lessons	Dates
1	Multiplicative Thinking	**4.OA.A:** Use the four operations with whole numbers to solve problems. **4.OA.B:** Gain familiarity with factors and multiples.	4 modules (Post module 3, Session 5)	• Postassessment by October 5 • TACA October 15
2	Multidigit Multiplication and Early Division	**4.NBT.B:** Use place value understanding and properties of operations to perform multidigit arithmetic.	4 modules (Post module 4, Session 5)	• Postassessment by November 7 • TACA November 19
	IAB for 4.OA (Questions 1–16) 4.OA Instructional Next Steps			
3	Fractions and Decimals	**4.NF.B:** Build fractions from unit fractions.	4 modules (Post module 4, Session 4)	• Postassessment by December 19 • TACA January 14
	IAB for 4.NF (Questions 1–10) 4.NF Instructional Next Steps			
4	Addition, Subtraction, and Measurement	**4.NBT.A:** Generalize place value understanding for multidigit whole numbers. **4.NBT.B:** Use place value understanding and properties of operations to perform multidigit arithmetic.	4 modules (Post module 4, Session 4)	• Postassessment by February 1 • TACA February 11
	IAB for 4.NBT			

5	Geometry and Measurement	**4.MD.C:** Geometric measurement: understand concepts of angle and measure angles.	4 modules (Post module 4, Session 3)	• Postassessment by March 8 • TACA March 18
	IAB for 4.G			
6	Multiplication and Division, Data and Fractions	*Use of an efficient mathematics strategy (or series of strategies) to solve:* **4.OA.A:** Use the four operations with whole numbers to solve problems. **4.MD.A:** Solve word problems involving measurement and time.	4 modules (Post module 4, Session 3)	• Postassessment by April 19 • TACA April 29
	IAB for 4.NF (Questions 11–15) 4.NF Instructional Next Steps IAB for 4.OA			
7	Reviewing and Extending Fractions, Decimals, and Multidigit Addition	**4.NF.A:** Explain fraction equivalence and compare fractions with unlike denominators. **4.NF.C:** Understand the relationship between fractions and decimals, add and subtract to the tenths and hundredths.	4 modules (Post module 4, Session 3)	• Postassessment by June 1 • TACA June 10
	IAB for 4.NF			

Source for standards: NGA & CCSSO, 2010b.

Source: White River School District, 2019. Used with permission.

Figure 4.17: Grade 4 mathematics pacing guide.

that contains essential standards, learning targets, and formative assessments? Those are common questions for singletons in PLCs. Consider the example of a career and technical education teacher. At White River, Amy Miller, the college and career readiness director, oversees and provides support for CTE teachers and programs. Every Monday during collaboration time, you'll find Amy and the CTE teachers in the library. They are all singletons. They are, however, still expected to determine essential standards. CTE teachers start by examining their industry standards and pruning them down to what is essential. They receive time to reach out to a CTE teacher in another district who teaches the same course, or to connect with teachers who are part of their career and technical service organizations (CTSOs). These conversations give them a place to start when determining what's essential in their course or courses. School leaders encourage them to look at the assessment blueprint connected to the industry-recognized CTE certifications linked to the course. Teachers also have the opportunity to meet with industry advisory partners. Teachers give the industry advisors a list of their essential standards and ask for feedback. If students meet these essential standards, they should have the skills necessary for an entry-level position in the career field.

These singleton teachers are also bound together by committing to an English language arts standard—for example, an informational standard in writing like the following literacy standard from the Common Core State Standards (W.9–10.2.A):

> Introduce a topic; organize complex ideas, concepts, and information to make
> important connections and distinctions; include formatting (e.g., headings),
> graphics (e.g., figures, tables), and multimedia when useful to aiding
> comprehension. (NGA & CCSSO, 2010a)

The CTE team chose this standard because when it asked its industry advisory partners to weigh in on a writing standard to focus on across all areas, they responded that students need to be able to write an email to inform or persuade. Such conversations and processes bring clarity to what's essential, course by course.

White River CTE teachers are also linked by instructional strategies that include preteaching vocabulary. The team spends time discussing ways to teach and assess vocabulary. Members commit to coming together to analyze their data surrounding vocabulary on the end-of-unit assessment. Quarterly, they analyze the results of writing an email (based on a topic in their content area) to inform or persuade, which they score with the English language arts rubric. This CTE team of singletons has made a commitment to bring work and data to the table that reflect achievement toward the standard. The team members also spend time working on developing their unit plans, which include the essential standards, learning targets, success criteria, quick formative checks for understanding, and an end-of-unit assessment. They analyze and share their content-specific data with the college and career readiness director.

Another approach to collaboration is vertical teaming. What if a small school has only one sixth-, seventh-, or eighth-grade mathematics teacher? If these teachers work together in a collaborative team, they create a middle school mathematics team. Here's what their collaboration would look like: each teacher would come to collaboration time with data or student work that reflects the targets that were essential for students to learn that week. The sixth-grade teacher would share areas in which her students did well, what instructional strategies helped them, and what targets the students struggled to learn. The seventh- and eighth-grade mathematics teachers would discuss and model instructional strategies that could help students who are still struggling. The seventh- and eighth-grade teachers would then share their data and student work.

Conclusion

Teacher teams are where the collaborative work and impact on student learning is highly visible. The collaborative efforts at all levels of the district empower the work of these teams. The systemness of the work ensures alignment across the district by grade, as well as vertically. Positive change is driven laterally across the system. These teams collaborate to create a guaranteed and viable curriculum.

Coherence occurs when there is a shared depth of understanding about the practice of effective teaching and learning. It's when there's focused direction, intentional learning, collaborative cultures, and layers of accountability. A key aspect of this work is internal accountability. Every team takes ownership of the work at hand.

Chapter 5

Envisioning an Aligned District

Throughout this book, we have tried to paint a picture of a high-performing PLC district in which PLC practices and processes are aligned from the boardroom to the classroom with specificity and fidelity. Being able to visualize what a high-performing PLC district looks like is an important prerequisite for doing the right work—creating a vision of what your district seeks to become.

As we have attempted to show, developing such structures begins with the school board and superintendent team. This team makes a strong commitment to ensuring high levels of learning for all students and commits to implementing the concepts and practices of the PLC process as the primary approach for improving student learning and enhancing the professional satisfaction of administrators, faculty, and staff.

The school board and superintendent team clearly and frequently communicates a mission of ensuring high levels of learning for all students for success beyond high school, as well as a collaboratively developed and clearly articulated vision of the future. Importantly, the team has articulated meaningful commitments its members are willing to make in order to embed the district mission deep into every aspect of the district's structure and culture. As a result of in-depth data analysis that paints a portrait of the district's current state, the team sets both long-term strategic goals and short-term attainable goals, and frequently recognizes and celebrates success.

Creating a strong school board and superintendent team requires an effective superintendent. This should not be a surprise to anyone. We know the importance of effective classroom teachers for positively impacting student learning, as well as the importance of an effective principal in leading the school. As we have shown, the same is true for superintendents and school districts. Significant and effective districtwide efforts to improve student learning cannot be achieved with a weak or ineffective superintendent.

While the school board and superintendent team leads the collaborative processes that form the foundational why along with the direction for districtwide initiatives, it is the district leadership team that collaboratively develops the specific procedures and behaviors that result in a sharp focus on high levels of learning for all students across every aspect of the district culture. The district leadership team creates the conditions for a districtwide focus on improving student success across the district. To this end, the team's work is data driven; that is, its work addresses specific needs that team members identify in their collaborative analysis of student learning data, along with other indicators, such as the quality of adult work products.

The work of the district leadership team targets specific issues as needing attention, so the team engages in collective inquiry to identify the most promising approaches for addressing each issue. In other words, identifying best practices is more than a Google search or simply averaging the opinions of everyone on the team.

Importantly, the district leadership team is structured to function as a model for other teams throughout the district. The team collaboratively develops norms and shared commitments about how it will function. For example, team members set the structure for meetings and agendas and the overarching decision-making process based on the idea of "Would these decisions be good enough for my own child?" This is the "standard of care" that forms the philosophical underpinning of decision making at every level within the district.

The district leadership team links the school board and superintendent team with the principals. The building leadership team links the principals to the teachers. The building leadership team serves as a model for the collaborative teacher teams within the building, providing direction, support, monitoring, and celebration of progress.

The work of the building leadership team mirrors the work of the district leadership team in other ways. Members anticipate issues and questions, share learning data from each collaborative team, and practice the work that they will ultimately expect teacher teams to undertake. In short, the building leadership team team guides the work of enhancing student success throughout each building by leading and coordinating the work of teacher collaborative teams.

Grade-level and content-area teacher collaborative teams are the engine that drives the work of a high-performing PLC. These collaborative teacher teams use a cycle of continuous inquiry to answer the four critical questions of a PLC, ensuring learning for all students they serve. In a district-aligned PLC, collaborative teams use the same tools to do the same work across the district to provide a guaranteed and viable curriculum for students— regardless of which teacher they have and which school they attend.

Imagine being a new principal entering a district that is deeply engaged in the work of a PLC. Whether the principal is new to the role or has had many years of experience, he or she would notice how different the district and the schools within it function compared with a traditional school district, where each school operates independently and learning is up to chance. Imagine being a new teacher in such a district. The support and process structures in place within the school and district would allow every teacher in every school and classroom to provide a guaranteed and viable curriculum for every student.

If such a district as the one we have described in this book seems rather Pollyannaish, that means a worthy question to ask would be, "How many school districts would it take to convince us that it is possible to embed the concepts and practices of the PLC at Work process throughout an entire district with specificity and fidelity?" The answer should be "Only one." It can be done, and White River School District is evidence of that. So, for district leaders, the only questions left to answer are, "Why not us? Why not now?" It takes will and commitment, but you, too, can align your district PLC and reap the reward of increased student achievement and the professional growth of educators.

References and Resources

Ainsworth, L. (2004). *Power standards: Identifying the standards that matter the most.* Englewood, CO: Advanced Learning Press.

Ainsworth, L. (2010). *Rigorous curriculum design: How to create curricular units of study that align standards, instruction, and assessment.* Englewood, CO: Lead + Learn Press.

Bailey, K., Jakicic, C., & Spiller, J. (2014). *Collaborating for success with the Common Core: A toolkit for Professional Learning Communities at Work.* Bloomington, IN: Solution Tree Press.

Bayewitz, M. D., Cunningham, S. A., Ianora, J. A., Jones, B., Nielsen, M., Remmert, W., et al. (2020). *Help your team: Overcoming common collaborative challenges in a PLC at Work.* Bloomington, IN: Solution Tree Press.

Bezos, M. (2011). *A life lesson from a volunteer firefighter* [Video file]. Accessed at www.ted.com /talks/mark_bezos_a_life_lesson_from_a_volunteer_firefighter on May 4, 2020.

Bottoms, G., & Schmidt-Davis, J. (2010, August). *The three essentials: Improving schools requires district vision, district and state support, and principal leadership.* Accessed at www.sreb.org /sites/main/files/file-attachments/10v16_three_essentials.pdf?1459947461 on August 29, 2020.

Buffum, A., Mattos, M., & Malone, J. (2018). *Taking action: A handbook for RTI at Work.* Bloomington, IN: Solution Tree Press.

Chenoweth, K. (2015). Teachers matter. Yes. Schools matter. Yes. Districts matter—Really? *Phi Delta Kappan, 97*(2), 14–20.

Chenoweth, K. (2017). *Schools that succeed: How educators marshal the power of systems for improvement.* Cambridge, MA: Harvard Education Press.

Childress, S. M., Doyle, D. P., & Thomas, D. A. (2009). *Leading for equity: The pursuit of excellence in Montgomery County Public Schools.* Cambridge, MA: Harvard Education Press.

Collins, J. (2001). *Good to great: Why some companies make the leap—And others don't.* New York: HarperBusiness.

Conzemius, A. E., & O'Neill, J. (2013). *Handbook for SMART school teams: Revitalizing best practices for collaboration* (2nd ed.). Bloomington, IN: Solution Tree Press.

Deutsch, L. (2017, October 2). *Is it better to write by hand or computer?* Accessed at www .psychologytoday.com/us/blog/memory-catcher/201710/is-it-better-write-hand-or-computer on May 4, 2020.

Donohoo, J., Hattie, J., & Eells, R. (2018). The power of collective efficacy. *Educational Leadership, 75*(6), 40–44.

Drive Learning. (n.d.). *What is "Significant 72"?* Accessed at www.drivelearning.org /significant-72.html on May 4, 2020.

DuFour, R. (2007). In praise of top-down leadership. *School Administrator, 64*(10), 38–42.

DuFour, R. (2015). *In praise of American educators: And how they can become even better.* Bloomington, IN: Solution Tree Press.

DuFour, R., DuFour, R., Eaker, R., & Karhanek, G. (2010). *Raising the bar and closing the gap: Whatever it takes.* Bloomington, IN: Solution Tree Press.

DuFour, R., DuFour, R., Eaker, R., & Many, T. W. (2006). *Learning by doing: A handbook for Professional Learning Communities at Work* (1st ed.). Bloomington, IN: Solution Tree Press.

DuFour, R., DuFour, R., Eaker, R., & Many, T. W. (2010). *Learning by doing: A handbook for Professional Learning Communities at Work* (2nd ed.). Bloomington, IN: Solution Tree Press.

DuFour, R., DuFour, R., Eaker, R., Many, T. W., & Mattos, M. (2016). *Learning by doing: A handbook for Professional Learning Communities at Work* (3rd ed.). Bloomington, IN: Solution Tree Press.

DuFour, R., & Eaker, R. (1998). *Professional Learning Communities at Work: Best practices for enhancing student achievement.* Bloomington, IN: Solution Tree Press.

DuFour, R., & Fullan, M. (2013). *Cultures built to last: Systemic PLCs at Work.* Bloomington, IN: Solution Tree Press.

DuFour, R., & Marzano, R. J. (2011). *Leaders of learning: How district, school, and classroom leaders improve student achievement.* Bloomington, IN: Solution Tree Press.

DuFour, R., & Mattos, M. (2013). How do principals really improve schools? *Educational Leadership, 70*(7), 34–40.

Eaker, R., DuFour, R., & DuFour, R. (2002). *Getting started: Reculturing schools to become professional learning communities.* Bloomington, IN: Solution Tree Press.

Eaker, R., Hagadone, M., Keating, J., & Rhoades, M. (2021). *Leading PLCs at Work® Districtwide Plan Book.* Bloomington, IN: Solution Tree Press.

Eaker, R., & Keating, J. (2008). A shift in school culture. *Journal of Staff Development, 29*(3), 14–17. Accessed at https://learningforward.org/wp-content/uploads/2008/06/A-Shift-In -School-Culture.pdf on May 4, 2020.

Eaker, R., & Keating, J. (2009, July 22). *Team leaders in a professional learning community* [Blog post]. Accessed at www.allthingsplc.info/blog/view/54/team-leaders-in-a-professional -learning-community on May 4, 2020.

Eaker, R., & Keating, J. (2012). *Every school, every team, every classroom: District leadership for growing Professional Learning Communities at Work.* Bloomington, IN: Solution Tree Press.

Eaker, R., & Keating, J. (2015). *Kid by kid, skill by skill: Teaching in a Professional Learning Community at Work.* Bloomington, IN: Solution Tree Press.

Eaker, R., & Sells, D. (2016). *A new way: Introducing higher education to Professional Learning Communities at Work.* Bloomington, IN: Solution Tree Press.

Elmore, R. F. (2004). *School reform from the inside out: Policy, practice, and performance.* Cambridge, MA: Harvard Education Press.

Fullan, M. (2005). *Leadership and sustainability: System thinkers in action.* Thousand Oaks, CA: Corwin.

Hairon, S., & Dimmock, C. (2012). Singapore schools and professional learning communities: Teacher professional development and school leadership in an Asian hierarchical system. *Educational Review, 64*(4), 405–424.

Hattie, J. A. C. (2009). *Visible learning: A synthesis of over 800 meta-analyses relating to achievement.* London: Routledge.

Hayes, M., Chumney, F., Wright, C., & Buckingham, M. (2019). *The global study of engagement: Technical report.* Accessed at www.adp.com/-/media/adp/ResourceHub/pdf/ADPRI /ADPRI0102_2018_Engagement_Study_Technical_Report_RELEASE%20READY.ashx on May 4, 2020.

Jakicic, C. (2017, May 22). *Are essential standards a part of the assessment process?* [Blog post]. Accessed at https://allthingsassessment.info/2017/05/22/essential-standards-and-the -assessment-process on May 4, 2020.

Kanter, R. M. (1999). The enduring skills of change leaders. *Leader to Leader,* 1999(13), 15–22.

Keating, J., & Rhoades, M. (2019, Fall). Stomping out PLC lite: Every school, every team. *AllThingsPLC Magazine,* 21–23.

Kullar, J. (2018, Fall). How do we get teachers to lead? *AllThingsPLC Magazine,* 26–27.

Lezotte, L. W. (2011). Effective schools: Past, present, and future. *Journal for Effective Schools, 10*(1), 3–21.

Marzano, R. J. (2003). *What works in schools: Translating research into action.* Alexandria, VA: Association for Supervision and Curriculum Development.

Marzano, R. J., & Waters, T. (2009). *District leadership that works: Striking the right balance.* Bloomington, IN: Solution Tree Press.

Mattos, M. (2019, September). *How to build a culture of collective responsibility [Seminar presentation].* RTI at Work Institute, Bellevue, Washington, September 23–25, 2019.

Muhammad, A. (2019). *Transforming school culture: The believers.* Accessed at https://globalpd .com/search/content/MTYzMg==/Njc4NjM= on May 4, 2020.

Muhammad, A., & Cruz, L. F. (2019). *Time for change: Four essential skills for transformational school and district leaders.* Bloomington, IN: Solution Tree Press.

Muhammad, A., & Hollie, S. (2012). *The will to lead, the skill to teach: Transforming schools at every level.* Bloomington, IN: Solution Tree Press.

National Governors Association Center for Best Practices & Council of Chief State School Officers. (2010a). *Common Core State Standards for English language arts and literacy in history/social studies, science, and technical subjects.* Washington, DC: Authors. Accessed at www.corestandards.org/assets/CCSSI_ELA%20Standards.pdf on March 5, 2020.

National Governors Association Center for Best Practices & Council of Chief State School Officers. (2010b). *Common Core State Standards for mathematics.* Washington, DC: Authors. Accessed at www.corestandards.org/assets/CCSSI_Math%20Standards.pdf on March 5, 2020.

Peters, T. (1987). *Thriving on chaos: A handbook for a management revolution.* New York: Knopf.

Peters, T. J., & Waterman, R. H. (1982). *In search of excellence: Lessons from America's best-run companies.* New York: Warner Brooks.

Podolsky, A., Darling-Hammond, L., Doss, C., & Reardon, S. (2019). *California's positive outliers: Districts beating the odds.* Accessed at https://learningpolicyinstitute.org/sites/default /files/product-files/Positive_Outliers_Quantitative_REPORT.pdf on May 5, 2020.

Reeves, D., & Eaker, R. (2019). *100-day leaders: Turning short-term wins into long-term success in schools.* Bloomington, IN: Solution Tree Press.

Saphier, J. (2005). *John Adams' promise: How to have good schools for all our children, not just for some.* Acton, MA: Research for Better Teaching.

Schmoker, M. (2004). Learning communities at the crossroads: Toward the best schools we've ever had. *Phi Delta Kappan, 86*(1), 84–88.

Schmoker, M. (2009). *Focus: Elevating the essentials to radically improve student learning* (2nd ed.). Alexandria, VA: Association for Supervision and Curriculum Development.

Sharratt, G. (2002). *Keeping on your feet: A collection of stories.* Wenatchee, WA: North Central Service District.

Sharratt, L. (2019). *Clarity: What matters most in learning, teaching, and leading.* Thousand Oaks, CA: Corwin.

Sinek, S. [simonsinek]. (2009a, July 25). *Achievement comes when you pursue and reach what you want. Success comes when you are in pursuit of why you want it.* [Tweet]. Accessed at https:// twitter.com/simonsinek/status/2843724865?lang=en on May 4, 2020.

Sinek, S. (2009b). *Start with why: How great leaders inspire everyone to take action.* New York: Portfolio.

Wallace Foundation. (2009, March). *Assessing the effectiveness of school leaders: New directions and new processes.* New York: Author. Accessed at https://www.wallacefoundation.org/ knowledge-center/Documents/Assessing-the-Effectiveness-of-School-Leaders.pdf on December 12, 2020.

Wallace Foundation. (2013). *The school principal as leader: Guiding schools to better teaching and learning.* Accessed at www.wallacefoundation.org/knowledge-center/Documents/The -School-Principal-as-Leader-Guiding-Schools-to-Better-Teaching-and-Learning-2nd-Ed.pdf on May 4, 2020.Williams, K. C. (2010). *Do we have team norms or "nice to knows"?* [Blog post]. Accessed at www .allthingsplc.info/blog/view/90/do-we-have-team-norms-or-nice-to-knows on May 7, 2020.

Wolcott, G. (2019). *Significant 72: Unleashing the power of relationships in today's schools.* Winneconne, WI: FIRST Educational Resources.

Index

A

accountability, 6, 57, 87, 88
active research, 88–90
ADP Research Institute, 16
Ainsworth, L., 43
Allpress, A., 103
assistant principals, 8, 49, 74. *See also* principals
autonomy/defined autonomy, 5

B

Bayewitz, M., 75
Bezos, M., 69
BLT (building leadership teams). *See* building leadership teams (BLT)
BLC (building learning coordinators). *See* building learning coordinators (BLC)
Bottoms, G., 17
Buffum, A., 88, 101
building leadership teams (BLT). *See also* teams
    about, 73–74
    and aligning the work of collaborative teams, 10
    clarity about the work, establishing, 83
    collective inquiry and active research and, 88–90
    conclusion, 90
    cyclical processes and, 9
    envisioning an aligned district and, 138
    healthy culture, building, 86–88
    layers of leadership and, 74–77
    leading the learning and, 82–83
    progress monitoring toward goals and, 84–85

teacher collaborative teams and, 73
team leader training and, 77–78, 81–82
building learning coordinators (BLC)
    about, 62–65
    district leadership teams and, 8, 49
Byrnes, J., 82, 104, 105

C

calendars
    example PLC tasks for the school on the district calendar, 39–40
    example purpose and definition page of district calendar, 36
    written plans and, 31
career and technical education (CTE) teachers
    district leadership teams and, 49
    singletons and collaborative work and, 133–134
celebrations
    basic assumptions about aligning the work of teams districtwide and, 6–7
    controllable variables and, 104–106
    district leadership teams and, 69–71
checks for understanding example, 116
Chenoweth, K., 1
Childress, S., 94
Chino Valley Unified School District, 44–46, 47
clarity
    basic assumptions about aligning the work of teams districtwide and, 5
    district planners and, 36
    establishing clarity about the work, 83
    expectations and requirements and, 18–19
    principal leadership and, 50

classroom environment, controllable variables and, 94

collaborative teams/collaborative teaming. *See also* teacher collaborative teams; teams

and basic assumptions about aligning the work of teams districtwide, 3

clarity of term, 5

collaborative team meeting process, 107–108

in a PLC, 17

and role of the team leader, 106–107

and unit plan skeletons, 108–111

and White River School District, 16–17

collective efficacy, 52

collective inquiry and active research, 88–90

Collins, J., 75

common formative assessments, clarity of term, 5

controllable variables

about, 93–94

celebrations and, 104–106

classroom environment and, 94

guaranteed and viable curriculum and, 94–95

instructional strategies and, 96–97

monitoring and analyzing evidence of student learning and, 97–98

monitoring and giving feedback on products and artifacts and, 100–101

SMART goals and, 95–96

time, support, and extension for learning and, 101–104

uncontrollable variables and, 93

Cruz, L., 15, 68–69, 86, 87

culture

building a healthy culture, 86–88

principal leadership and, 68

Curran, M., 124–126

Cushman, M., 70, 82

D

data

cyclical processes and, 9

example data response protocol, 98–99

monitoring and analyzing evidence of student learning and, 97–98

TACA process and, 23

defined autonomy, 5

differentiated teaming, 63

Dimmock, C., 73

district calendars. *See* calendars

district leadership teams (DLT). *See also* teams

about, 49–51

and aligning the work of collaborative teams, 10

building learning coordinators and, 62–65

celebrations and, 69–71

conclusion, 71

cyclical processes and, 8–9

envisioning an aligned district and, 138

essential standards and, 43

focused teamwork and, 65–67

knowing the work and, 56–60

principal leadership and, 67–69

principals as district leaders, 51

professional development and, 60–62

why and how, communicating, 52–56

district planners, 32, 36. *See also* planning/tools for planning

district, envisioning an aligned district, 137–139

districtwide planning process, 30–31. *See also* planning/tools for planning

DLT (district leadership teams). *See* district leadership teams (DLT)

Doyle, D., 94

DuFour, R., 2

DuFour, R.

on clarity, 50

on collaborative culture, 91

on collective inquiry and action research, 88

on goals, 85

on leadership teams, 78

on principal leadership, 71

on progress monitoring, 54

on impact of superintendents, 2

on role of principals, 50, 56–57

on systemness, 73

on taking responsibility, 42

on top-down leadership, 13

on work of principals, 57–58

E

Eaker, R.

on collaboration and planning, 29

on expectation-acceptance gap, 17

on impact of superintendents, 2
on principal leadership, 68
on student learning data, 97
on team leaders, 75
on unit planning, 123
Edwards, K., 56
Elmore, R., 6
end-of-unit assessment example, 116–118
envisioning an aligned district, 137–139
essential standards
    and guaranteed and viable curriculum,
        94–95
    and principals knowing the work
        deeply, 59
    and scaling the work, 43–44
    and unit plan skeletons, 108
    and unwrapping standards, 88–89
evidence of student learning, 97–98, 100–101
expectation-acceptance gap, 17
expectations and requirements
    about, 17–18
    clarity and, 5
    clarity and goals and, 18–19
    loose-tight leadership and, 19–20
    SMART goals and, 20–21
    TACA process and, 22–24, 29
    team meetings and, 21–22
extending the learning
    controllable variables and, 101–104
    critical questions of a PLC and, 16–17

F

feedback, controllable variables and, 100–101
focus on learning, 36
Fullan, M., 5, 73, 78

G

game ball celebrations, 104–105
Gelinas, L., 82
goals. *See also* SMART goals
    building leadership teams and, 84–85
    expectations and requirements and, 18–19
Gray, P., 97–98
guaranteed and viable curriculum
    controllable variables and, 94–95
    responsibilities of principles and, 57
    scaling the work and, 42–43
guiding coalitions, 2, 78

H

Hairon. S., 73
Harrison, S., 70
Hattie, J., 94
Hollie, S., 54
how, the, 54–55. *See also* why, the
how collaborative teams function. *See also*
        collaborative teams/collaborative
        teaming
    collaborative team meeting process
        and, 107–108
    role of the team leader and, 106–107
    unit plan skeletons and, 108–111

I

improving the learning/teacher collaborative
        teams. *See* teacher collaborative teams
In Praise American Educators (DuFour), 57–58
*In Search of Excellence: Lessons from America's
        Best Run Companies* (Peters and
        Waterman), 5
information flow, 62, 63
instructional strategies, 96–97
interventions and remediation, 16. *See also*
        RTI/MTSS process
introduction
    about districtwide school improvement, 1
    about this book, 9
    basic assumptions about aligning the work
        of teams districtwide and, 1–7
    conclusion, 12
    cyclical process, 8–9
    right work, the right way, for the right
        reasons, 7–8
    White River School District, 11–12

K

Kanold, T., 105
Kanter, R., 70
Karhanek, G., 2
Keating, J., 17, 24, 75, 97, 123
Keeping on Your Feet (Sharratt), 31
Kuntzelman, F., 107

L

layers of leadership, 74–77
leading the learning, 82–83

leading the work at the school level/building leadership teams. *See* building leadership teams (BLT)

learning targets, focused teamwork and, 65, 66

Lezotte, L., 1

loose-tight culture/leadership
  basic assumptions about aligning the work of teams districtwide and, 5–6
  expectations and requirements and, 19–20
  responsibilities of principles and, 57

M

Malone, J., 88

Markey, N., 69–70

Marzano, R., 1, 5, 42, 71

Mattos, M., 44, 88

meetings
  and attitudes toward teamwork, 24
  and building a healthy culture, 87–88
  collaborative team meeting process, 107–108
  and district leadership teams, 74
  and expectations and requirements, 21–22
  and focused teamwork, 65–67
  and leading the learning, 82–83
  and monitoring and analyzing evidence of student learning, 100–101
  and principals knowing the work deeply, 59
  RTI/MTSS meetings, 102–103
  sample building leadership team meeting agenda, 72
  sample district leadership team meeting agenda, 71

mission statements, 54

Mothershead, C.
  on collaborative team leader training, 78
  on expectations regarding the work, 109–110
  on monitoring progress and giving feedback, 100–101
  repeating process and, 83
  on understanding the work, 60

MTSS (multitier system of supports). *See* RTI/MTSS process

Muhammad, A.
  on change, 15
  on culture, 68–69, 86, 87
  on mission, 54
  on relationships, 94

multitier system of supports (MTSS). *See* RTI/MTSS process

N

norms, 87

O

observations, 58, 60

P

paraeducators, 74

Peters, T., 5, 6

pipeline issues, 53

planning/tools for planning. *See also* unit planning
  about, 29
  district calendars, 31
  district planners, 32, 36
  districtwide planning process, 30–31
  example district task page of the district PLC planning tool, 33–35
  example PLC tasks for the district office on the district PLC planning tool, 37–38
  example purpose and definition page of district PLC planning tool, 32
  hoping to planning, from, 29–30
  monthly planning tools, 122–123
  platform for transparent collaboration and, 118–119
  White River School districtwide plan book excerpt, 41

PLC (professional learning communities)
  collaborative teams and, 17
  critical questions of, 16–17, 61, 91–92
  impact of superintendent in, 2–4

PLC at Work process, impact of, 1

POP (proof of progress), 109–110, 114–115

power standards. *See* essential standards

Power Standards (Ainsworth), 43

principals
  basic assumptions about aligning the work of teams districtwide and, 3–4
  building a healthy culture and, 86, 87–88
  building leadership teams and, 74
  collective inquiry and active research and, 88–90
  communicating the how, 54–55

communicating the why, 52–54
connecting the why and how, 55–56
as district leaders, 51
district leadership teams and, 8, 49, 50
focus on principal leadership, 67–69
impact of, 56
knowing the work, 56–60
layers of leadership and, 74–77
professional development and, 60–62
responsibilities of, 57–58
team leader training and, 77–78, 81–82
professional development, 60–62
professional learning communities (PLC).
        See PLC (professional learning
        communities)
progress monitoring
        basic assumptions about aligning the work
        of teams districtwide and, 6–7
        building leadership teams and, 84–85
        communicating the how and, 54–55
        communicating the why and, 52–54
        controllable variables and, 97–98, 100–101
        professional development and, 60–62
        responsibilities of principles and, 57, 58
proof or progress (POP), 109–110, 114–115

R

Raising the Bar and Closing the Gap (DuFour,
        DuFour, Eaker, and Karhanek), 2
reciprocal accountability, 6, 57, 88
Reeves, D., 68
repeating process, 83, 84
response to intervention (RTI). *See* RTI/
        MTSS process
Rhoades, M., 24
Ross, J., 81
RTI/MTSS process
        about, 101–102
        critical questions of a PLC and, 16
        responsibilities of principles and, 58
        RTI pyramid, 102
        RTI/MTSS in action, 103–104
        RTI/MTSS meetings, 102–103

S

"Save the Shoes" award, 69–70
scaling the work, 42–46
Schmidt-Davis, J., 17
Schmoker, M., 5, 24

school board and superintendent teams. *See
        also* teams
        about, 13–14
        and aligning the work of collaborative
        teams, 10
        collaborative teaming and, 16–17
        conclusion, 46
        cyclical processes and, 8
        envisioning an aligned district and,
        137–138
        expectations and requirements and,
        17–24, 29
        scaling the work and, 42–46
        shared knowledge and, 14–16
        written plans, developing, 29–32, 36
school leadership team. *See* building
        leadership teams (BLT)
school-level teacher teams. *See* teacher
        collaborative teams
Schumacher, C., 64
Sells, D., 29
setting the stage/district leadership teams.
        See district leadership teams (DLT)
shared knowledge, building, 14–16
Sharratt, G., 31
Sinek, S., 4, 14
singletons and collaborative work, 126,
        133–134
SMART goals. *See also* goals
        controllable variables and, 95–96
        example first-grade SMART grade
        tracker, 96
        monthly planning tools and, 122–123
        process for establishing, 20–21
        setting SMART goals, 89–90
*Start with Why: How Great Leaders Inspire
        Everyone to Take Action* (Sinek), 14
starting at the top/school board and
        superintendent team. *See* school board
        and superintendent teams
summative assessments, clarity of terms
        and, 5
superintendents. *See also* school board and
        superintendent teams
        basic assumptions about aligning the work
        of teams districtwide and, 2–4
        district leadership teams and, 49
        impact of, 137
systemness, 73

T

TACA (team analysis of a common assessment)

   example form showing data protocol questions, 28

   example form showing graphed unit 1 reading tab results, 27

   example form showing Reading Class 1 formative tab, 26

   example form showing tab for Reading Class 1, 25

   example form showing unit 1 reading tab, 27

   expectations and requirements and, 22–24, 29

   monitoring and analyzing evidence of student learning and, 97

   monitoring team progress toward goals and, 85–86

teacher collaborative teams. *See also* collaborative teams/collaborative teaming; teams

   about, 91–93

   and aligning the work of collaborative teams, 10

   conclusion, 134–135

   controllable variables and, 93–98, 100–106

   cyclical processes and, 9

   envisioning an aligned district and, 138

   how collaborative teams function, 106–111

   singletons and collaborative work and, 126, 133–134

   tools for team planning and, 118–119, 122–126

teachers

   building leadership teams and, 74

   building learning coordinators and, 62–65

   career and technical education (CTE) teachers, 49, 133–134

   singletons and collaborative work, 126, 133–134

   teachers on special assignment (TOSA), 8, 49

teacher-student relationships, 94

team analysis of a common assessment (TACA). *See* TACA (team analysis of a common assessment)

team leaders

   building a healthy culture and, 86, 87

   building leadership teams and, 74

   collaborative team leader description, 76

   collaborative team leader-selection tool, 77

   collective inquiry and active research and, 88–90

   example leader training agenda, 81

   layers of leadership and, 74–77

   role of, 106–107

   team leader training, 77–78, 81–82

   team leader training current reality assessment tool, 79–80

team meetings. *See* meetings

teams. *See also specific teams*

   basic assumptions about aligning the work of teams districtwide and, 1–7

   Chino Valley's collaborative team actions simplified in a PLC at Work tool, 47

   differentiated teaming, 63

   resources and support and, 6

terms, clarity of, 5

Thomas, D., 94

tiers of intervention. *See* RTI/MTSS process

time, support, and extension for learning, 92

tools for team planning. *See* planning/tools for planning

top-down leadership, 13

U

Uhler, C., 110–111

unit planning. *See also* planning/tools for planning

   district-developed resources for unit planning, 123–126

   example geometry unit plan, 111–114

   example grade 4 mathematics pacing guide, 132–133

   example grade 4 mathematics unit plan, 127–132

   unit plan skeletons and, 108–111

unwrapping standards, 88–89

Upham, G., 55–56

V

Vail, K., 86, 106

variables. *See* controllable variables

vertical teaming, 134

W

Wallace Foundation, 56, 67, 73
Waterman, R., 5
Waters, T., 1, 5
White River School District
    collaborative teaming at, 16–17
    implementing PLC at Work concepts and
        practice, 11–12
    information flow in, 63
why, the. *See also* how, the
    basic assumptions about aligning the work
        of teams districtwide and, 4–5
    connecting the why and how, 55–56
    principals and, 52–54
    shared knowledge and, 14–16
Why Tour, 55
Work, The
    about, 119
    example elementary The Work site home
        page, 119
    example resources for teachers and teams,
        120
    example school PLC folders, 121
    example state standards by grade and
        content area, 120
    example unit plan skeletons and common
        assessments, 121
    example with data that show the overall
        student achievement levels from each
        school, 122
written plans. *See* planning/tools for planning

“I came to the presentation pretty much devoid of an understanding of how the **Common Core** was going to affect my students and my instructional methods. I walked away **excited** and feeling **validated.**

I'm on board!”

—David Nohe, teacher,
New Mexico School for the Blind and Visually Impaired

 PD Services

Our experts draw from decades of research and their own experiences to bring you practical strategies for integrating the Common Core. You can choose from a range of customizable services, from a one-day overview to a multiyear process.

Book your CCSS PD today!
888.763.9045

Solution Tree

Learning by Doing
Richard DuFour, Rebecca DuFour, Robert Eaker,
Thomas W. Many, and Mike Mattos

Discover how to transform your school or district into a high-performing PLC. The third edition of this comprehensive action guide offers new strategies for addressing critical PLC topics, including hiring and retaining new staff, creating team-developed common formative assessments, and more.
BKF746

A Summing Up
Robert Eaker

After a career spanning nearly half a century, Dr. Robert Eaker delivers a work of reflection and storytelling. Learn from a master educator as he shares the story of his career, along with in-depth guidance for implementing the PLC at Work® process.
BKF943

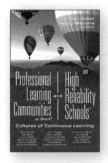

Professional Learning Communities at Work® and High Reliability Schools™
Cultures of Continuous Learning
Edited by Robert Eaker and Robert J. Marzano

Dramatically improve schooling by harnessing the collective power of the High Reliability Schools™ (HRS) model and the PLC at Work® process. Featuring some of America's best educators, this anthology includes information, insights, and practical suggestions for both PLCs and HRS.
BKF938

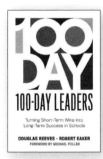

100-Day Leaders
Douglas Reeves and Robert Eaker

Within 100 days, schools can dramatically increase student achievement, transform faculty morale, reduce discipline issues, and much more. Using *100-Day Leaders* as a guide, you will learn how to achieve a series of short-term wins that combine to form long-term success.
BKF919

Every School, Every Team, Every Classroom
Robert Eaker and Janel Keating

The PLC journey begins with a dedication to ensuring the learning of every student. Using many examples and reproducible tools, the authors explain the need to focus on creating simultaneous top-down and bottom-up leadership. Learn how to grow PLCs by encouraging innovation at every level.
BKF534